HOW TO BREAK
THE GLASS
CEILING

And Still Keep it Nice

An Anthology of Shared
Wisdom For Women Executives

Edited by Lil Barcaski, Linda Hinkle, and Teresa Selby Fink

Published by: Center of Influence Publishing
www.centerofinfluencecommunity.com

Cover Design: Kristina Conatser and Mindy Scarlett

ISBN: 978-1-959608-43-1

Dedication

We dedicate this book to the trailblazing women who carved the way for us. To the new generation of female executives, we hope you, too, will soar high above the "proverbial" glass ceiling, and we hope that the following generation will be saying "What glass ceiling?"

Contents

Foreword

The term "climbing the corporate ladder" is believed to have originated in the mid-20th century, specifically during the 1950s and 1960s. This phrase became popular as a metaphorical expression to describe the process of advancing in one's career within a hierarchical corporate structure.

The phrase "breaking the glass ceiling" was coined in the late 1970s and early 1980s. It is often attributed to Marilyn Loden, who used the term during a panel discussion on women's career issues at the 1978 Women's Exposition in New York. Loden used the metaphor of a glass ceiling to describe the invisible barriers that prevent women from reaching top-level positions in male-dominated professions or organizations.

The term gained widespread recognition and popularity in the 1980s as a powerful symbol of gender inequality and the challenges women face in their professional advancement. It has since become a rallying cry and a call to action for gender equality and breaking down barriers to women's success in various fields. The concept of the glass ceiling has sparked conversations, research, and initiatives focused on dismantling gender biases and creating more inclusive work environments.

I firmly believe that with determination, perseverance, and the support of allies, women can break through the glass ceiling and achieve success in their careers. Climbing the corporate ladder as a woman is not without its challenges, but it is a journey that is both rewarding and empowering. By embracing ambition, building a strong network, developing confidence, engaging in continuous learning, and navigating gender biases, I have been able to make significant strides in my career.

It is my hope that by reading our stories, other aspiring women can find inspiration and the tools they need to succeed in their own professional journeys. Together, we can shatter the glass ceiling and create a more inclusive corporate world for generations to come. (Wouldn't it be wonderful if the next generation did not even know what a glass ceiling was?)

Mindy Scarlett
Co-Founder, Center of Influence Community
www.centerofinfluencecommunity.com

Ericka Dunlap

After fulfilling her childhood dream of becoming Miss America in 2004, Ericka has gone on to explore many other paths from the music industry to being a corporate board member. She is currently the CEO of the Crown Communication Group, providing unique PR services to her clients.

Finding the RIGHT Ladder to Climb!

by Ericka Dunlap

I was lucky that I discovered what ladder I wanted to climb when I was six years old! My first career began when I got involved in the beauty pageant industry and discovered that I loved it. Here I was as a young girl, able to get up on a stage and command an audience, be creative and just have fun in a way that was completely foreign to most of my fellow first grade friends. As a child, I was very inquisitive, introverted and academically inclined. Team sports were not of interest to me, and although I was enrolled in vocal lessons, tap, jazz, and ballet classes, I only mildly enjoyed other group activities.

With pageantry, I was able to compete against myself with each competition. What exactly does that mean? Well, I learned early on that the politics of pageants were out of my control. There was nothing that my parents nor I could do to influence the judge's scoring, manipulate the pageant directors into selecting me or any other clever tactic to win the competition other than present the best version of myself on stage. It was me against my last performance! I enjoyed m Remember, my degree is in PR odeling in the various fashion categories, being interviewed by the judging panel and presenting my talent, which at the time was dancing. The dif-

ferent competitions encouraged me to develop a positive awareness of my self-image as well as the important value of sportsman-
ship. Even at that tender age, I found myself reading everything I
could get my hands on to help me prepare for each next competition. That was when I knew that I wanted to get to the very top of
this particular ladder—I knew I wanted to go all the way to Miss
America.

Learning how to "lose like a winner" and having the ability to extend congeniality by congratulating competitors who advanced
over me has left an indelible impact on my life. As you get clear on
the ladder that makes the most sense for you, remember to play
nice along the way. I took a break from the pageantry world during
high school and in college I returned to my ladder of choice. It was
the second semester of my freshman year in college at the University of Central Florida when I started to get really serious about
this particular ladder of pageantry. I took being in pageants very
seriously because it greatly impacted my funding for college. Specifically, to the credit of the Miss America Organization, I have
never faced a student loan! Whew!

Throughout my entire pageant career, I won over $200,000 in
scholarships, which also paid for my off campus living expenses, a
new computer each year (if I chose), books and meal plan. In fact,
it was during my freshman year that much of my hard work paid
off when I was crowned Miss Orlando and awarded $12,000 in
scholarships. For context, the first Miss Florida Pageant was held
in 1922, and it would be for another 48 years before Black Women
were legally permitted to compete for the title. Knowing this history, I was more energized to keep climbing the ladder! I competed for 3 years, placing in Top 10 for the first two years, and then
when I was a Junior in college, I became the first African American
woman to win the coveted title of Miss Florida!

Now, winning at the state level was significant, because that put me
on the path to go to the big competition – Miss America. However,
it was also significant on another level, because my win represented something that was actually illegal for Black Women to pur-

sue until 1970, which included my grandmother, my mother, my aunts, and a host of other Black women who were major influences on my life. This meant a lot not only for me, but also for the legacy of young women who would aspire to compete and win, while benefiting from my breaking of that particular glass ceiling.

Climbing this particular ladder taught me many things. First and foremost, pageantry is not just glitz and glamour, it's fundraising! Business development, relationship building, and resource management are essential and underrated elements of the business, even down to assembling the right team of coaches and consultants who can help you to accomplish the next goal. I think most people expect pageants to be superficial, like you put on a pretty dress and parade around for people to choose you as the prettiest girl in the bunch, but there's a great deal of discipline, preparation and money that has to be raised and put into this package for the odds to work in your favor.

Once I knew I was officially headed to the Miss America competition, I carefully built my team around me. I did not want to be someone's puppet, just parroting what other people told me to do and say. My confidants were a sacred source of daily motivation and challenges. I was determined to make this part of the climb up the ladder on my own terms. My team helped me do just that, and I was crowned Miss America 2004 on the iconic 50ft runway in Atlantic City's Boardwalk Hall—I had reached the top of the ladder!

Thus began an amazing year of completing my duties as Miss America, which included delivering over 100 Keynote Addresses, conducting media junkets almost daily, and traveling every 48 hours to a new city for appearances and meetings. The most fulfilling of all, was the opportunity to travel to Kuwait and honor the US military servicemen and servicewomen during Thanksgiving. Wow! My dream had come true at age 22!

THE NEXT LADDER

After a dynamic and challenging year as Miss America, I then had to pick the next ladder to climb. I wanted to continue to pursue the creative aspect of what I had enjoyed in the pageant circuit, so I went toward a career in entertainment, which was yet another learning curve. Singing had been my talent all through the pageant circuit, I decided to "take a run at" Nashville and Country Music. One month after I graduated with my bachelor's degree in Public Relations & Advertising, I packed up, moved to Tennessee and began the process of launching my singing career.

It was exciting to be in a new city, meeting new people and having a chance to really stretch my singing talent and begin planning for a new career. I did everything I could to immerse myself in the Music City culture! I went to songwriting sessions, open mic nights, artist showcases, and lots of concerts. Each week, I met a new person who wanted to help me, and it was my job to weed out the ones with their own selfish ambitions, yet another aspect to be aware of when climbing your perspective ladder.

What people don't often realize is that launching a singing career is basically about being self-employed. You must learn the business, figure out how to position yourself, and market the product: yourself! I really enjoyed singing, I was very good at it, but I was NOT an expert in the music business!

At the time, I was coming off the heels of earning a massive salary from Miss America. I was determined to invest that money in the next phase of my career. However, I could not seem to get to the finish line of actually of making money from the music industry. It became very bittersweet to pursue my dream and my goal, because I was not seeing the return. After six years, I decided to recalibrate and move back to my hometown.

CORPORATE LADDER, HERE I COME!

My first experience with the corporate ladder happened when I accepted a paid internship.

This was a highly desirable position for a local Public Relations Firm with national reach. I anticipated collaborating with the Associates and Partners on important media plans, high profile events and developing data-rich white papers. To my chagrin, I was actually expected to file papers and go on coffee runs. Nearly 10 days of meaningless frappe orders, and I knew this was a match made in hell! It was in this moment that I reminisced on a precious conversation with one of my Mentors where she emphatically expressed, "If something is not a hell yes, it's a hell no!" This internship was a definite hell no!

In that very brief time, I developed a horrid disdain for the office environment and particularly for my overinflated, micromanaging supervisor. Each time I parked my car in its designated spot, my body encountered a visceral response. I intuitively knew that my skills would not be utilized or sharpened in this space, and I vowed to myself to NEVER work anywhere again that did not fully align with my intuition. On day 10, I was scheduled to go into the office, but instead, I submitted a definitive notice of resignation, effective immediately, and I never looked back!

However, fast forward a few years and once I decided that the music industry and I were not mixing well, I decided to jump back on the corporate ladder. This position was with an IT firm based in California, and I was charged with the goal of creating the PR department. I had a lot of autonomy and it seemed like a good fit for the first eight months. It was at this point that my director resigned from the company and there was no one to take her place. I was new to the company and working remotely in Florida. Battling the different personalities and the office politics of the people who were in California became a huge issue, and it began to affect my quality of life. That is what helped me to finally jump on my own ladder and become an Entrepreneur.

Although Entrepreneurship is celebrated and glorified, let me tell you, it is NOT for the faint of heart! You must be committed and unwavering in your belief in yourself and relentless in organizing your ideas. Successful entrepreneurs obsess about their business. They are disciplined and resolute, and they take the painful steps up each rung of that ladder to make it happen.

MY OWN LADDER

After this final experience with the corporate ladder, I finally decided it was time to build my own ladder! So, in 2014 I launched my own Public Relations firm called Crown Communication Group. I started out with two clients who were old friends, and they had some really great opportunities for me. They helped me establish confidence in my ability to create a business and grow my expertise to meet the demand that was out in the marketplace. Remember, my degree is in PR, so, I knew what to do and how to do it, but my first few clients served as the foundation for me to understanding my business of my business — the finances, the nuances, and the challenges. One such challenge that I was forced to overcome early on was tackling the "budget boutiques." These competitors in the industry would offer a skimmed down monthly program that diluted the potential client's understanding of the investment. These other PR shops would suggest a few social media posts per week and a press release or two for a monthly fee of nearly free! Crown Communication Group was founded with the mission to put a crowning touch on your bottom line, which does not come cheap. Redefining my company's offerings and finding my niche was vital to taking the next steps on my ladder. Similar to my first career in pageantry, I had to block out the competition and put all of the focus on my next best performance for my next client. It was all up to me to outdo my last project and to carry out the four P's of Public Relations: Protect, Promote, Perform and Prove.

After my first four years into surviving Entrepreneurship, I took another leap of faith on my ladder and endeavored another star in my crown (pun intended) when I decided to create a co-working space for women entrepreneurs. I wanted to provide the ultimate environment for women who were start-up entrepreneurs to find an affordable office space and be able to conduct their business in a feminine and suitable environment that helped them to present their business professionally. I found just the right space, carefully curated the furniture and the office design, and hung out the sign. I had quite a few supporters and lots of women who were coming in. They would use the space as a day office, or use the conference room to sign contracts, or they would hold strategy meetings in the event space. It was a beautiful location that was specifically designed for women to feel comfortable in.

However, the Universe had other ideas, when March of 2020 arrived and along with it came Covid-19 and a complete quarantine and lockdown. So, I had to close my carefully curated shared workspace, put all the furniture in storage and go back to the drawing board about what ladder I was going to be on next! This was very painful, both personally and professionally. I really felt I was making a difference for women entrepreneurs, and I had invested quite a bit of money into creating that special and unique environment for them.

I guess Mother Nature decided to get together with the Universe and create even more surprises for me, as I suddenly discovered that I was pregnant. While this presented some unique challenges, I decided that I would continue my work with my company and work from home, as I was forced to close my office along with the shared workspace. Surviving through Covid while pregnant with my first child at the ripe age of 38 was the ultimate challenge, but I was determined to stick with the ladder of my choice – being an Entrepreneur!

WHICH LADDER IS RIGHT FOR YOU?

To be an Executive Woman, you must first make the decision as to which corporate ladder you wish to climb. This is a significant choice that can have a profound impact on your personal life as well as your professional career. Are your skills and ambitions best served in the C-suite, as an Executive Board Member, or perhaps as an Entrepreneur and Chief Executive of your own operation? Perhaps you are interested in impacting your community in the non-profit space or you may have your eyes set on a top spot at a large organization. While each of these paths has its benefits and drawbacks, taking inventory of all of your best professional assets will give you the confidence needed to take the next steps.

When it comes to climbing the corporate ladder (and breaking the glass ceiling!) your journey and your climb only needs to make sense to you, and it is critically important that you select the right corporate ladder, structure and culture that best suits your values, lifestyle, personality and skill sets. As you take your first few steps along your climb, there are some key factors that impact your rise including personal growth, skills development, cooperation with other people and communication style.

According to USChamber.com, the C-suite leaders are considered the highest level of the organization (unless there is a Board of Directors). These leadership positions include: Chief Executive Officer, Chief Operating Officer, Chief Information Officer, Chief Financial Officer, Chief Diversity Officer, and Chief Marketing Officer. There are other executive job titles that are close to the same function as these C-level positions, but don't have "chief" in the name. For instance, President, Partner, Chair and Superintendent are other titles that can be found at the top of the org chart. These individuals manage the day-to-day operations of the business to maintain profitability and overall market success.

The Board of Directors are the distinguished governing body of a company who share insights and resources to set strategy and manage oversight. Board Members, (also may be referred to as Directors or Governors) are qualified professionals that are not direct employees of the company, but offer expertise in an associated area and are well-versed in the inner workings of an organization.

The primary job of The Board is to provide corporate oversight and approve C-suite management policies. From making decisions on stock dividends to setting executive compensation, and even hiring and firing of senior-level executives—a Board of Directors fulfills a variety of roles that help hold a company accountable to those with a vested interest in its success. How a Board of Directors governs differs from organization to organization, and the way it operates is set out by a company's bylaws. Bylaws affect everything from setting the number of board seats to establishing a cadence for meetings, setting election procedures and more.

I had the privilege of becoming a paid Board Member for a wonderful organization and it came about quite by accident! It all started when I attended an Alumni fundraising event, where I had the pleasure of meeting a group of interesting individuals who also attended my university from various generations. Little did I know that this encounter would lead to a remarkable journey of networking, learning, and making a significant impact as an Executive Board Member.

As I chatted with these newfound acquaintances over the table, I didn't realize that this was more than just a social gathering. Sometimes, it can be easy to dismiss and disregard networking events, especially for introverts. However, this was the perfect chance to step outside of my natural comfort zone and seize the moment by nicely chatting and finding common ground. It was an opportunity to expand my network and open doors to unforeseen possibilities. One of the people I met was a man who graduated in 1981, the same year I was born! What struck me was his willingness to believe in my potential. He recognized my unique skill set and expertise, and he saw the diverse perspective and value I could bring to his organization. It was a pivotal moment where someone had faith in me and my capabilities. At the end of the conversation, he invited me to begin the process to become a paid board member for his organization.

The organization he invited me to be a part of focused on prescription fulfillment for Veterans. Serving as a Board Member, I discovered a new realm of responsibility and influence. It was no longer just about being an employee; it was about being a voice at the decision-making table. I realized the power and responsibility that came with the position. Being on the Board provided me with invaluable learning experiences. I gained insights into effective board governance, strategic planning, and resource management. I became more adept at bringing resources to the organization and amplifying its profile. The impact I could make as a Board Member far exceeded what I could accomplish as an employee alone.

Our organization's primary mission was to provide Veterans with the medications, medical supplies, and prosthetics they needed without financial burden. It was deeply fulfilling work, knowing that we were making a tangible difference in the lives of those who had served our country. Advocating for their needs and ensuring their well-being became my passion. Sadly, after a year and a half of dedicated service, the organization decided to dissolve the board due to the sale of the company. It was a bittersweet ending to an incredible chapter. However, the experiences and lessons I gained during that time will forever shape my perspective and professional journey.

As I reflect on this unique experience, I realize that being a Board Member opened my eyes to new possibilities. It served as another rung on the ladder of career growth. I learned the importance of seizing unexpected opportunities, building connections, and leveraging my skills in unconventional ways. From a chance meeting at a fundraising event to becoming an effective Board Member, my journey taught me the power of networking, the belief in my potential, and the impact one can make in a leadership role. It emphasized the significance of continuous learning, amplifying the profile of an organization, and serving a fulfilling purpose. As I continue on my career path, I will always cherish the experiences gained from being a Board Member and remain open to the next ladder that comes my way, ready to embark on new adventures and make a difference in whatever capacity I can.

If you are more inclined to be in control of your own ladder, then Entrepreneurship is the way to go. Entrepreneurship is the process of creating and managing a new business venture in order to make a profit. It requires a high level of creativity, risk-taking, and problem-solving skills. Entrepreneurs are usually self-starters who are driven by their passion for their business idea and their desire to be their own boss. They have to be willing to take on financial risk, work long hours, and adapt to changing market conditions.

A Forbes.com article entitled, "Why Entrepreneurship is one of the most versatile survival skills," suggests that entrepreneurial thinking goes beyond starting companies and running small businesses. This particular skillset is also equally valued at large corporations to drive product ideas and innovation processes. The rewards of entrepreneurship can be remarkable, including the potential for limitless financial success, personal fulfillment, and the ability to create a meaningful and lasting legacy through a brand.

One of the key factors that can influence the decision to go corporate or be an entrepreneur is personality. Entrepreneurs tend to be risk-takers who are comfortable with uncertainty and ambiguity. They are often highly motivated, driven, and passionate about their business ideas, and they have a strong desire to be their own boss and have control over their work environment. In contrast, those who prefer a more structured and predictable work environment may be better suited to working in the corporate space. They may be more risk-averse and prefer the stability and security that a corporate job can offer.

Financial considerations are also a significant factor in the decision to go corporate or be an entrepreneur. Starting a business requires a significant investment of time, money, and resources. Entrepreneurs must be willing to take on debt or invest their own money in order to get their business off the ground. In contrast, working in a corporate environment offers a more stable income and benefits, which can provide financial security.

Another important consideration is the level of independence you desire. Entrepreneurs have a high level of independence and control over their work environment. They are responsible for making all decisions related to their business, from hiring employees to setting prices. However, this level of independence can also be a double-edged sword, as entrepreneurs often have to bear the brunt of any failures or setbacks. In contrast, working in a corporate environment can provide a sense of security and stability, but may also limit an individual's independence and creativity.

At the end of the day, it is important to find just the right ladder. In order to do that, you need to really examine who you are as an individual, what makes you happy and where your "super powers" are concentrated. And, like me, you may have to experiment with different ladders before you find the one that is "just right"!

> *"No matter how you feel —*
>
> *Get up. Dress up. Show up.*
>
> *And NEVER give up."*
>
> ANONYMOUS

The quote above is one that is very near and dear to my heart. I have found that reciting and reflecting on affirmations are of very high priority to my daily routine. Each time I glance at the phrase, the words impress fresh meaning to me. The simple, yet profound quotation aligns my discipline into action when I feel like throwing in the towel. The phrase has encouraged me on the days when Imposter Syndrome and comparison has snuck into my mind and I just didn't feel like showing up as "The Queen of Everything" — the decision maker, the risk taker, the one who always figures it out, whatever "it" may be. And this is a great quote to keep in mind when trying to determine what ladder you should climb, and once you decide on the right vertical, how you are going to face your future.

First take a look at the initial declaration, "No matter how you feel." The statement succinctly blocks self-sabotage and negates excuses. Why is this important? Because feelings are temporary! Period. Good feelings come and go, just as bad feelings come and go. Along your journey as an Executive Woman, you must remain laser-focused on controlling your emotions and communicating with tact and resolve.

Next, "Get up." Literally, get up and hop to it! Allow your purpose to be your alarm clock! Dismiss depression and get moving! Quiet down anxiety and imposter syndrome with intentional movement, exercise, dancing, stretching, breath work, affirmations, meditation, prayer, etc. Commit to at least one or any combination of these activities first thing in the morning as a foundation for the day ahead. Get up and say nice things to yourself! Get up and admire your beauty and your battle scars! Get up and do something thoughtful for yourself that will enhance your day!

Next, "Dress up." Dressing for success has a key affect to one's mood and productivity. In this context, I interpret the phrase as referring to a clean, coordinated, well-fitted and appropriate clothing selection rather than a formal and fancy designer outfit. The only requirement to this declaration is that you must dedicate time to prepare yourself for the type of image that you wish to project and do so consistently. When you take the time to invest effort into your clothing selections, ensuring that your garments are clean, wrinkle-free and properly fitting, then you will better value the concept of getting dressed as an extension of your reputation.

Last, but certainly not least, this quote charges you to "Show up," which is likely the most difficult task of them all. Showing up requires you to take the decisive action to go for it! And, this can be scary.

In summary, finding the right ladder to climb is a journey. Find ways to enjoy the process and be gentle with yourself. No one has a perfect formula, and just know that if it is meant to be yours, nothing can stop it from getting to you. Most importantly, never give up and never give in. No matter which ladder you choose to climb, there will be challenges and obstacles. But remember, if the dream or goal is in your heart, then you will be equipped to handle the pressures and pivots that come with it all.

To better discover your executive brand, the team at Crown Communication Group would love to connect and schedule a consultation. We specialize in helping busy professionals to optimize their professional presence and put a crowning touch on your bottom line. Connect via social media or our website at:

www.crowncommgroup.org

Cornita A. Riley

Cornita's career in corrections spans almost four decades and after retiring as chief of Orange County (Florida) Corrections in July 2018, she decided to utilize her extensive years of leadership experience by launching a consulting firm called Motivating People to Rise Higher. Cornita is passionate about providing leadership training and development for those desiring to develop or improve their leadership skills, particularly for women.

Leadership, Being First and Paving the Way for Others

by Cornita A. Riley

Having passed retirement age, I have exhausted most of life's professional firsts. My parents and older siblings considered me a "miracle baby" because I was the only baby of many stricken by dehydration diarrhea to survive, coming out of a "colored" hospital in St. Petersburg, Florida. I grew up the youngest of six children, two boys and four girls. The one thing I always knew was that we were loved and constantly affirmed and encouraged to become all we desired to be. When I first started grade school, I was very quiet, shy, and introverted. As time went on, like many awkward teens, I finally found my footing and found my voice.

Although I was not the first of my siblings to attend college, I was the first girl to graduate. My family was immensely proud of me and genuinely celebrated my accomplishments. After graduating from Florida State University, I returned home and quickly acquired a job as a social worker. I believe deeply in purpose and the pursuit of purpose. Truly believing we are created to serve others, I strived to serve my community long before the term servant leadership was coined. This belief has manifested itself in my life, both personally and professionally.

When reflecting on the name of my initial place of employment, Florence Nightingale, I feel like it was a bit foretelling. I found I had a true calling for serving others and for doing what I could to help others identify their strengths and aspirations, and then help them chart a way to fulfill their God-given purpose. I really enjoyed my work as a social worker, but I quickly learned that my deep commitment, dedication, and engagement with my clients and their families created too much pain when a client passed away. After the death of my third client, I decided to find a different job—one in which I could serve others, help make a positive difference in their lives, and still be personally fulfilled in what I did for a career.

I did not realize it then, but attending a Christmas party and meeting someone who worked for the Department of Corrections (DOC) was a major turning point in my professional life. This person simply thought I would do well in that organization. I don't even know why they said it other than they knew the department was looking for new hires. And so, that's what led me to Corrections, and how I started my new career as a field services, probation, and parole officer.

Once in this new arena, I found a passion for something that I could do well, and I truly believed that I had found my niche. After a few years, I met an exceptional young man who was also working for DOC in another region. We got married and relocated to Polk County. I was able to transfer with DOC, but relocating led me to a new discipline. I began working in what was referred to as the "Court Team," on behalf of the Corrections Department.

This position really captured my attention and was a total game-changer. I was given the opportunity to help pilot and evaluate the first sentencing guidelines implemented in the state of Florida. I understood the importance of having accurate information in the pre-sentence investigations. The sentencing guidelines scoresheet was created primarily from the information collected in these investigations. (The courts use scoresheets to determine a person's sentence.) Thus, I realized the value of the work our agency was responsible for, and I understood that my role played a critical part in this work.

However, even as I found great fulfillment in my position with the "Court Team," I began to witness and experience my first instances of what appeared to be biased treatment based on both race and gender. So much so, that I found myself advocating for a young man I knew was being mistreated solely because of the color of his skin. It was the first time I found myself acting in the role of an informal leader, doing what was right because I knew I had a duty to do so.

This led to findings of discrimination by some of the leaders in the office where this young man worked. He was finally taken care of and treated with the dignity and respect he deserved, and those responsible for inappropriate actions and behavior were held accountable. This was just the first of a few negative and biased experiences I encountered while in that region, but I am not one who will ignore an injustice. I will always stand up for what is right, fair, or just.

I believe I always knew there would be roadblocks and challenges for me as a double minority (female and African American). Not only was there still a lot of pushback against minorities, I was also a female, working in a male-dominated profession. I believe I was also a bit naïve because I hadn't personally encountered any of these biases in my first couple of years with the DOC. I realized later how blessed I was to have started this career working with progressive and fair-minded supervisors.

After realizing the magnitude of the negative environment we were working in, and having had our first son who was now a toddler, we decided to sell our home and relocate to Orlando. While my husband stayed with probation and parole, I chose not to stay in that arena and applied for positions in other areas of Corrections.

This is where my career took a turn, and it was only years later that I could look back and see how pivotal this one decision was for my career. I transferred from being a probation and parole field officer to being a classification officer (working title) working within a prison environment. I quickly found my new niche helping the incarcerated population see the value of being involved in self-betterment programs.

I found myself in a position where I could now put the pieces together. I had done field services supervising probationers. I had done investigations, creating the pre-sentence and post-sentence investigations. I had worked with the court in creating the scoring sheets for sentencing. Now, on the other side, after a person is incarcerated, in classification, I began to use another set of instruments and tools to establish the potential risk level that a person poses both inside a prison and when they are released.

So, now I was putting all these pieces together and I was fascinated. I was interviewing and creating internal program plans for individuals that were incarcerated. And when they were getting ready to be released, I created a release plan and connected the dots on what their needs were both internally and externally (when they got out). I found myself making significant inroads in helping that population. I helped them recognize what they needed to "own" in terms of their criminal history, but also talked with them about their dreams, their goals, and how to change and create a positive life outside the walls of the prison. I found myself back in a significant counseling role, showing them how getting out can be a new beginning.

Here's the funny thing, the classification officer position was not the position I really wanted. I wanted to be an inspector in the Inspector General's Office. However, during this time within the DOC, there was little desire for married females to serve in this capacity. As a matter of fact, when I did interview for a position as an inspector, I was asked, "How do you think your husband would feel about you working with a male inspector on a case that might require staying overnight somewhere?" I kind of chuckled and said, "Well, I don't think my husband would feel any differently than he feels now when I'm out and about without him."

I thought about it for another moment or two, and then I finished my response with, "Well, I guess I would also have to ask you, how do the wives of the male inspectors feel when their husbands are out overnight with one of the two single female inspectors you currently have?" to which one of the interviewers responded "Touché!" While I did not get this position, it felt good to stand up for myself as a female, and I had made the three-man panel aware of their bias.

Over the next few years, I was promoted to classification supervisor at the same prison. I was again very passionate about my role, and about the roles our unit played in the service of that population. I believe it was at this time that I really began to see the impact I could have within the DOC. I found myself enjoying coaching and counseling, with both the incarcerated population and the staff in my unit.

The warden became a mentor of sorts for me. I was inspired by the way my warden served with such command presence yet, with great compassion and commitment. (The warden greatly influences the dynamics at any given institution.) I began to see myself leading in that role; ensuring that my team understood the mission of every correctional facility: "care, custody, and control." I realized I needed to chart a new course because I wanted to become a warden.

The next promotional opportunity proved to be the next instance of both biased (or unfair) decision-making and courageous leadership. I applied for a mid-level manager position. If successful in obtaining this promotion, I would lose my status as a "department head," but moving to a larger prison would position me for other opportunities in the future. This was the next defining moment in my career, as a Black female working in this male-dominated profession.

One of the minimum requirements of this new position was for each of the applicants to be a "certified probation officer" at the time of application. There were about thirteen applicants for this position, and of those that were offered an interview, one was not a "certified probation officer." Clearly, this person should not have competed in this promotional process. Nevertheless, not only did this applicant compete for the mid-manager level position, but they were selected and promoted to it.

Eventually, I received a call from a fellow applicant who told me about the violation in the hiring process. I was asked to join a "class action" grievance. I didn't feel that strongly about the situation, so I chose not to join. I later discussed the matter with another colleague and mentor who gave me some very good advice. They advised that if I was not personally aggrieved by the decision that was made, I should be careful about taking on other people's battles. They went on to share that I had a reputation of being fair, open-minded, approachable, reasonable, and, as such, I needed to be careful regarding the battles I choose take up and fight.

Here is the irony. As time passed, I, and likely all the other applicants, received a call from the regional director apologizing for what had occurred regarding the promotion process. He went on to say that the process was being redone and, if interested, I should expect a call for a new interview. Although the person who was initially given the promotion had obtained her probation officer certification, she was temporarily reassigned to another position.

So, the new interviews were set up. This warden was a man from the North Florida area. The second interview went well, and as the warden requested, I went to meet with him. He proceeded to explain to me that it would not matter whom I might have talked to, or who chose to talk to me, it was his decision who was going to work in his institution, and no matter how I felt about it, "yada yada, yada." Bottom line was, he seemed offended that he had been required to remove his initial selection from the position and redo the interviews. About two weeks later, I was promoted to that mid-manager position. Although I was a little apprehensive about accepting the promotion, I decided not to allow someone else to determine my future. So, I packed my things and reported to my new institution and assignment.

This was a major culture shock for me as I learned that three-quarters of the staff were not from the Central Florida area but were transferred from North Florida. And so, all the mentality and culture of North Florida came to Central Florida, and there were some real disconnects in how management worked with staff. I point this out only because, it's critically important that those in leadership understand how "culture" can and does impact the work place. It's important for those in leadership to understand everyone they work with, bring different cultural experiences, perspectives, and values to the workplace. As such, a leader's responsibility is to communicate the mission and values of the agency, their alignment with their unit, and to make clear the expectations regarding the duties and responsibilities of the work to be performed. It is also their responsibility to recognize the value that each person bring to the workplace, utilize their strengths and respect all staff, regardless of their race, sex, ethnicity, or background.

In this new work location, there was an older male supervisor who was the department head. His style of leadership was like a bull in a China shop. So much so that when staff would hear him coming down the hallway, they would run and duck into restrooms or behind doors until he had passed so they could avoid interacting with him. They made jokes and thought it was funny, but I looked at this and said, "How in God's name could this man have been successful in his career with that type of demeanor?" I thought it was horrifying, and I tried to understand how this behavior had been tolerated for so long!

Then there came the day that his vitriol was aimed at me. After the first incident, I went in and requested a meeting with him. We sat down and talked, and I explained to him that I thought his behavior toward me was highly disrespectful, that I would never disrespect him or anyone else that way, and I expected the same in return. "We can agree to disagree, but we must agree that you don't get to yell and scream at me. I'm a grown person. And I don't even speak to my children the way that you speak to the staff in this department." He apologized to me and said "Oh, that's, you know, that's just my personality. That's the way I come off. I don't mean anything bad." To which I replied, "Well, your way doesn't work for me. It shuts me down and limits my ability to do what I'm here to do. And I know that it's offensive to the staff because they have also talked to me."

Not long after that, this same supervisor chose to burst into my office, literally screaming at the top of his lungs. I decided then and there this was the last time he was going to disrespect me. It was clear this man's behavior had been tolerated for so long that he couldn't change it. It was clear that it was time to take this to the top because all intermediate attempts had failed. Thus, I met with the warden, which I considered an official filing of the problem. The warden, whom I had the utmost respect for, listened attentively and, at the end of our conversation, assured me the situation would be addressed. To my complete surprise, the "bull" was demoted several levels and transferred back to North Florida, where he eventually retired.

It caused an interesting stir when I was promoted to fill his position. False rumors that I had engineered the entire thing to get his position had begun to spread. However, I had learned long before to ignore such whispers–I knew in my heart that the motivation for my actions was to de-escalate a very disrespectful and negative situation and to create a positive work environment. This was necessary, not only for me to work in a more stress-free and productive environment, but for the other supervisors and staff as well. I considered being promoted to this department-head-level position a testament to my leadership style and the positive reputation I had developed.

My next significant assignment was when I was tapped to lead the DOC in implementing the principles of total quality management. I knew this was going to be a mammoth undertaking as the agency was huge, spanning the entire state of Florida. In this role I found myself having to identify a cross-functional team of staff, and I was deliberate in ensuring they were diverse in race, gender, and ethnicity. I was given full support from my supervisors and offered opportunities to develop my own knowledge, skills, and abilities in ways that would benefit me, not only in my current assignment but also in my overall development as a leader.

My team and I were successful in developing a relationship with Mayport Navel Training Station and we negotiated a contract between the Quality Management (QM) Training Department and DOC[BJ1] . This was the very first military/Corrections partnership of its kind. This served as a huge boost to my career as a leader in DOC. I believe it is important to acknowledge that it was a female who headed up Mayport's QM program. She made herself available to assist me in navigating the culture of the military in order for us both to achieve a positive outcome. To this day, we are still colleagues and friends.

Another major breakthrough for my career, and an opportunity to help advance other women in the DOC, came when I was selected to be on a team of women who would help develop and implement a training program called "Women Facing the Future." This assignment ignited the desire in me to do all I could to help women understand the importance of recognizing their value and not compromising their integrity for any promotion. My area of expertise sharing while with this training program was, "Building Self Esteem." Sharing my story was cathartic for me and for the women who had encountered some of the same or similar challenges while striving to crack this particular glass ceiling.

Over an eighteen-year period, I was promoted from correctional probation officer to supervisor, to assistant warden and finally to regional assistant warden for Administrative Services, reporting to one of five regional directors. I traveled throughout my region, which was comprised of approximately thirteen prisons, work camps, and work release centers. I was offered and earned opportunities that many others did not have. I believe I was extremely blessed. I found favor with my superiors, whom were all males.

They were truly instrumental in helping me accomplish my goals and my dreams.

Additionally, I found myself doing what I believe all good leaders do—helping staff identify their goals, their strengths, and areas for improvement. I found myself identifying and advocating for professional development training and programs for staff. Reflecting, I believe this was an example of servant leadership at its best. I believed in modeling what I encouraged in others: a solid work ethic, an awareness of self, strengths, areas for improvement, respect for everyone regardless of their place in life—and above all, being non-judgmental. One of my philosophies in life really is, "There, but for the grace of God, go I."

The way my parents raised my siblings and me instilled a lot of positive and strong values in each of us. Values like respect for others and the fact that, regardless of our differences, we each have worth and something valuable to share with others. I also found myself being effective in getting people to recognize and, in many cases, accept responsibility and accountability for their actions and non-actions.

Of course, this wasn't always the case. That's when (I believe) great leaders know how to demonstrate tough, yet humane communications. Another one of my philosophies is this: when leaders have tough conversations with staff, it's important to do it with respect and to ensure staff leave the conversation still "standing" with their dignity. I genuinely think that this type of leadership leads to staff being more committed to doing and giving their best.

It is my passion for what I do that propels me to always ask, What is the next step? What is the next level for me to achieve that will help make a positive difference? It has never been about having power or authority for me. I recognized that, most of the time, the ability to influence change was in direct proportion to where you sat in the chain of command.

It was then that I faced a serious crossroads between my career and my family. I had to decide if I would potentially create havoc in my family by accepting an appointment to my dream job of warden. Well, I choose my family. This was another lesson along my journey that I would later share and help guide other women when they faced making this same decision. My decision may not be the right one for everyone but, I didn't believe it was necessary to compromise my relationship with my family and create undue hardship on our family unit for a promotion. And because I didn't, at the exact right time, an opportunity appeared that allowed me to transition from the DOC to the Orange County Corrections Department (OCCD) with Orange County Government.

While I had definitely not set my sights on becoming deputy chief of Corrections for Orange County, the opportunity presented itself when it had been determined that the agency had grown enough to warrant having two deputy chiefs. However, the chief at the time wasn't inclined, initially, to consider me for one of the two positions. Instead, he wanted to put forward two men for deputy chief positions and forward my name and request for another new position, just under the deputy chief level. However, when this scenario was presented to the powers that be, it was rejected. As such, I was appointed, as the first female (who also happened to be Black!), to deputy chief of the OCCD.

While still reeling from my new assignment, my excitement was quickly dashed by the reality of gender and potential racial bias. Although I did not seek what my male counterpart was being paid, office gossip soon caught up with me and revealed that I was being paid less. I experienced a range of emotions, none of which were good. And though I don't believe there was any real intent to devalue my worth, I did feel devalued.

I was able to voice my concerns to my supervisors. I assured them that I was very appreciative of the opportunity, but when my credentials and experience were lined up with those of my male counterpart, mine were clearly more extensive and more diverse, yet he was being paid more. By choosing the diplomatic route to address this inequity, I was once again able to effect a positive change without having to file a formal complaint. I do believe those in leadership are more effective when they can find positive, non-threatening ways to negotiate positive change. As an aside, it's interesting to note that, there was a female at the executive level, who for some reason was offended that I had brought forward the inequities in our pay. Just because there may be a female in high places, it doesn't mean you may not have to fight for fair and just treatment.

After serving for almost a decade as deputy chief, I had the opportunity to be appointed as the first female Chief of Orange County Corrections, who again, happened to be Black. Being appointed by the first female "County Mayor" was truly apropos. This marked yet another significant first in my career in this male-dominated profession.

HAVING A SEAT AT THE TABLE

I am very proud of helping pave the way for so many other women and people of color, and ensuring that these groups were, at the very least, offered a seat at the table. Looking at the bigger picture, not only were minorities missing from the room and from the table, but in many cases, they weren't even given an opportunity to compete for higher level positions. I became acutely aware of the behind-the-scenes tactics that were often used to keep certain groups of people from elevating within the organization.

I felt it was imperative to start respectfully calling these situations out while requiring our Human Resources (HR) departments to do their job. I made it clear that part of their job was to help ensure the agency lived up to what we said we were, an equal opportunity employer (EOE). I brought HR staff into the room with my leadership team and explained who we were supposed to represent, which was a microcosm of the community at large. I made my expectations regarding our recruitment and hiring processes very clear. We evaluated all position descriptions for accuracy and made updates as appropriate. I required that I be involved in all position postings and assessment processes until I was assured that the processes we were utilizing was, in fact, reflective of the best we could do, and the processes were fair and equitable across the board. As the chief of the agency, I knew I needed to be involved, and stay involved, until it was clear that we were all operating from the same set of expectations. This was a far bigger undertaking than I ever imagined.

I worked with my department to develop a full recruitment team, with new paraphernalia and literature. All print and media materials reflected the diversity of the organization and the many career opportunities offered in Corrections. I charged our HR Department with ensuring our recruitment team became visible at all job fair opportunities within the region, and I made sure they were sent to local and out-of-state conferences. The OCCD recruitment team became the talk of the profession, as they were sharp in appearance, intellect, and resource materials. This was one of my proudest moments, and it still brings me joy when I reflect upon how much we accomplished.

Looking back over the eighteen and a half years in Orange County, I am proud of my work. Some of the most defining moments during my journey started when I was promoted from major/manager to deputy chief to chief of Corrections. In each of these positions, I became the first-ever (Black) female to serve at those levels of responsibility and leadership. I often felt people looked at me as if I were a unicorn! During my tenure as chief, I was instrumental in ensuring several other females were elevated to key leadership positions. I am proud that I could help them find the cracks in the glass ceiling.

When looking back over my career as a leader, and looking forward in my new endeavors, I fully embrace and understand the importance of servant leadership. My top three takeaways for successful leaders include:

1. Leaders must be present and actively engaged with their people. They must be visible and available; approachable and willing to listen, not just giving orders and issuing directives.

2. Leaders must provide clear communication regarding their vision and the path to accomplish that vision. Leaders must be able to communicate clear expectations and ensure staff have the necessary resources to achieve the expectations, tasks, and goals they have been given; and to undertake actions that will keep staff motivated and engaged. And finally,

3. Leaders must understand the importance of responsibility and accountability. Demonstrating accountability for their own actions and decisions, both good and bad, reveals a leader's ability to focus on everyone's success and not just their own. It shows their ability to be vulnerable and fallible, yet courageous and strong in character and integrity. I truly believe it was best said by Arnold H. Glasow, "A good leader takes more than his[/her] share of the blame, a little less than his[/her] share of the credit."

I retired from Orange County Corrections in July 2018. In the process of preparing for retirement, I was offered an opportunity to begin doing some consulting work in leadership development for women already in leadership positions. One of my very first projects was a yearlong assignment, working with women in leadership at Rikers Island. Aside from consulting with other companies, I also formed my own limited liability company (LLC) called MPRH—Motivating People to Rise Higher. My focus is leadership development, with an emphasis on helping women develop strong leadership principles and skills.

One of my favorite quotes is from poet Maya Angelou, "Your legacy is every life you've touched." I wanted to share my story to illustrate that it is possible to rise as a woman in a male-dominated profession, and not compromise who you are, your family and still maintain your femininity. It became important to me to build a legacy worth passing on.

What I hope is that part of my legacy is encapsulated in a quote from Andrew Thorn, "Leadership is the act of making things better for others." I believe I can say, I was able to create a few cracks in the glass ceiling. I contend there is still much work to be done in many traditionally male-dominated positions, but women are making great strides in many of these professions. We must always be willing to serve as mentors, role models, and "trail blazers," bringing others along with us as we pave the way for more to follow.

CORNITA A. RILEY is a 44-year veteran in the criminal justice field, specifically in the area of Corrections. She retired as chief of Orange County Corrections (Florida) in July 2018. She is the founder and manager of Motivating People to Rise Higher Consulting Firm, which specializes in leadership development. She is also an adjunct instructor for Valencia College School of Public Safety. She is passionate about providing valuable leadership training and development for criminal justice professionals, particularly for women. She is a graduate of Florida State University and earned her master's in public administration from the University of Central Florida.

Book an appointment to chat with me to discuss how I can help you with your organizational leadership needs and get access to my top leadership tips and resources via:

https://cornitariley.com

Dr. Donna Smith Bellinger

Dr. Donna Smith Bellinger is a highly accomplished CEO and sales consultant with over 40 years of corporate leadership experience. As the CEO of DS Bellinger Consulting, LLC, she brings a wealth of knowledge and expertise to help her clients drive impressive results.

Creating your Own Economy Through Negotiations, Sales and Relationship Building

by Dr. Donna Smith Bellinger

I never would have imagined that my life would turn out quite the way it did. In the beginning, my life seemed very straightforward. It was a comfortable existence in the suburbs outside of Chicago, where I went to private school, and had opportunities to travel. I was an only child with seemingly every opportunity. However, everything changed at age 15 when my parents got divorced.

My father remarried and I suddenly found myself part of a blended family. No longer the center of attention and in defiance of my new circumstances, I began acting out, making several bad decisions. At 17, guess what – I was pregnant and of course my family did not approve. Their prediction was that I would end up working on the streets in six months. They showed me the door with a six-week-old.

So, I went from living in the suburbs, being in private school, and having the support of my parents, to being a single parent with no home, no money, completely on my own. The first and most imperative lesson (learned the hard way) was how to handle money. I remember having a very spirited discussion with a bank teller over a check that was returned for insufficient funds and arguing with them about not processing the check. "Miss Smith, there is no money in your account," they explained. My response to them was, "But I still have two boxes of checks left." My sheltered life had not taught me about banking and economics!

After holding several entry level positions, I decided to go back to school and explore my passion for technology. While the experience was wonderful, something even better was in store for me. After completing my program, I was offered an amazing opportunity, and became the school's first assistant director of admissions at just 21 years old.

How did I get where I am today? The answer is simple: hard work, determination, and a willingness to learn from my mistakes. My journey wasn't easy, but it was worth it. Over the years, working in vocational education and corporate sales, and the lessons gained and opportunities that followed changed the direction of my life. Fortunately, there were people that entered my life that saw things in me that I did not see in myself, and I was always coachable. Despite many challenges, I bootstrapped my way through business and management to eventually co-found a successful tech firm. Eventually becoming a certified business and entrepreneurship coach, adjunct, consultant, trainer, speaker, and business author.

BUILDING YOUR OWN ECONOMY

To become the boss of me, I have learned how negotiation, sales, and relationship building are essential skills for success in any field. It has been shown that successful professionals of all types become successful because they think like business owners, regardless of who writes the check. Yes, there were many challenges in my career. I've often been underestimated because of my gender and race. I have overcome those challenges by leveraging my strengths, showcasing my value, and making myself memorable, whether I was working for myself or for someone else.

I've shared my expertise on big stages, podcasts, tv, radio, and in print. My family represents four nationalities and five generations. We are African American, Italian, Italian-Irish, Mexican, and LGBTIQA+. Because of this, I am very focused on communication and creating my own economy to build a better future for my grandchildren and their children after them. This is the world they will inherit.

To grow, it has been necessary to turn my fear into confidence, and that is a vital skill I transfer to my teams and clients. While making money is important, I don't believe that it is right to make money by any means necessary. My core value was one of service and sharing. My personal mission statement is: "The work I do must affect more than a corporate bottom line"—it had to make a difference. When that piece is in alignment, regardless of the product or service I represented, I could do anything.

Building a successful career or business requires more than just working on the business. To be prepared for opportunities, you also need to work on yourself and become an entrepreneur or executive who stands for something. The best business people I know have a fundamental desire to help people. Their service or product is how they deliver on that desire.

As I continue my journey as a sales trainer and coach, I am committed to helping others shorten their learning curve to successful outcomes and take control of their economy. By mastering negotiation, sales, and relationship building, we can break the glass ceiling and unlock unprecedented opportunities for advancement.

THE NEED TO UNDERSTAND THAT SALES IS A PROCESS

Sales doesn't have to be hard. It's not some magical talent that only a few possess. I have many years of experience helping professionals become high performers.

It's a process that you can learn, understand, and master.

Sales is not about pushing products or persuading others against their will. It's about building genuine connections, understanding the needs of your clients, and offering them a solution that will enhance their lives. Creating your own economy is not about a passive "wait and see" approach; it requires proactive action and a mindset geared toward rapid results.

What are some strategies for making sales less scary and either growing your business or extending your reach as an executive?

1. **FOCUS ON THE PROBLEM YOU'RE SOLVING:** Don't talk about all the fun features, or how you learned to do XYZ, because ultimately nobody cares. Instead, focus on how your product or service will make their lives better or address their current challenge. What changes can you bring that will make their lives easier? Will they save money? Make more money? Save time so they can be with their family more? What is the goal your product/service will achieve for them?

2. **LEVERAGE YOUR EXISTING CONTACTS:** You don't know who they know and what opportunities are out there. As a member of the National Alliance of Market Developers, I would often visit a Chicago Public access tv studio to watch our weekly live broadcast (my husband loves that kind of thing). One week the host failed to show up. The producer looked at me and said "Donna, you're on!" I hosted the program for a year and I had no idea those types of opportunities were out there for me.

3. **SHIFT YOUR MINDSET AND APPROACH:** Sales is not about being pushy or aggressive. Instead, focus on service rather than sales. By shifting your mindset and approach, you can make sales conversations more comfortable and effective. Every firm I ever represented had their own style of sales training that focused primarily on two things: features and benefits, not the needs of the client. In order to stay sane (and in integrity), I developed a different style for communicating with my prospects that became my trademark. Attendees of my workshops learn my process for pre-qualification and refusal aversion (not conversion) as a part of developing their personal sales communication styles.

4. **UNDERSTAND YOUR CLIENTS' NEEDS:** Building genuine connections and understanding your clients' needs is key to successful sales. Listen to your clients and ask questions to understand their pain points and needs. Then, offer them a solution that addresses those needs.

5. **DON'T WAIT:** Time waits for no one, and neither should we when it comes to our financial success. Waiting for the right moment or the perfect opportunity will only delay your progress. Be persistent and take control of your revenue (your personal economy) and processes to achieve your goals.

Remember, sales is an opportunity to be of service and make a positive impact on your clients' lives. By focusing on the problem you're solving, shifting your mindset, understanding your clients' needs, and acting, you can make sales less scary and grow your business.

WHEN THE CONCEPT OF SALES MAKES YOU ITCH!

There really isn't that much difference between top earners and average earners. The difference is in their motivation, focus, and perseverance. To overcome any reservations you may have, start by reframing your perspective on sales. Embrace the notion that it is an opportunity to make a positive difference in people's lives. When you view sales as a means of service, it becomes a more fulfilling and authentic endeavor.

Additionally, remember that control plays a pivotal role in sales. Not that "hit you over the head ego" driven control, I mean that you have the power to shape your success, drive your revenue, and create the life you desire. This control enables you to establish comfortable working relationships with your clients, knowing that you are providing them with high value and solutions tailored to their needs. Rise above any discomfort associated with the word "sales" and reframe it as an opportunity to serve others genuinely. You can harness the power of conversations that convert, to reclaim control over your revenue and processes, and make a lasting impact on the lives of your clients. It's time to transform your perspective, step into your true potential, and embark on a fulfilling journey of sales and service.

Fear of failure? As a sales professional, I've come face-to-face with countless objections. They are like roadblocks standing in the way of achieving an enthusiastic "yes" from potential clients. We all know that "yes" is the ultimate goal. So how can we handle objections effectively and navigate the challenges of virtual communication? Let's dive in.

One common roadblock we encounter is when prospects say, "I have to think about it" or "I'm already working with someone." It's disheartening when these objections arise because they seem like dead ends. However, this is not the end of the conversation. We must anticipate and address these concerns head-on and further demonstrate the value of our products or services.

To counter the objection of needing more time to think, we need to help prospects understand the cost of inaction. I often ask clients, "How much money are you losing by not resolving the issue that my product or service will solve?" This question prompts them to consider the implications of their current challenges. It might be costing them time, affecting their health, or success in their career path.

By highlighting the impact and quantifying the potential benefits, we demonstrate that the cost of not acting far outweighs any perceived financial investment. Objections may seem like insurmountable hurdles, but with the right approach, they can be overcome. By highlighting the cost of inaction and quantifying the benefits, we address potential clients' concerns effectively.

THE POWER OF LISTENING AND EFFECTIVE COMMUNICATION

Let's face it, we've all encountered challenges in our careers and businesses. We've heard objections, faced rejection, and second guessed ourselves, wondering what we should be doing differently. But here's the truth: it's not your fault, you are not broken and you don't need fixing. All you need is a little more focus and a few additional tools to succeed.

What hasn't kept pace is the training we receive. Most companies fail to update their training programs to align with the realities of today's virtual world. They neglect to equip us with the skills needed to thrive in this new era. One crucial aspect of successful sales conversations is tailoring them to the other person, whether this is a peer, employer or even your family. And the best way to do that is to learn the art of listening and apply effective communication.

One of my most requested talks is "Communicating across Gender, Generation & Geography" which clearly demonstrates the conscious and unconscious blocks we create for ourselves as well as how subtle changes have a great impact in outcomes.

YOU LOST ME @ HELLO

The opening chapter of my book, *You Lost Me @ Hello: Actionable Principles That Move You Beyond Networking* states "Not everyone will need you. So please don't generalize who you are seeking to connect with. It's not, 'people with money,' 'people of influence,' or that kiss of death 'Everybody!' A lesson I learned with experience (aka 'age') is not only will I not be liked by everyone, but I don't want everybody to like me.

"That's far too time-consuming. How many events can you attend, calls and emails can you return, and how many other people's feelings can you worry about?

"Get a handle on what you truly want to achieve and create a plan that is inclusive of your values, your talents, and your interests."

It's about listening more and talking less. I understand this can be challenging, especially for those who are accustomed to being an expert in the room.

It's vital to recognize that clients don't want to be overwhelmed with a tsunami of information and they most definitely are not going to retain most of it. The client wants someone who is savvy, understands their needs, and can offer relevant solutions when appropriate. That's where your listening skills come into play. When engaging with clients, take the time to truly listen.

Ask probing questions to uncover their pain points and desired outcomes. Consider asking them, "What would an ideal situation look like for you?" or "What is the cost of not addressing this challenge?"

By understanding their perspective and goals, you can better align your offerings and tailor your approach to their specific needs. Furthermore, effective communication goes beyond your interactions with individual clients. It extends to how they choose to introduce you to their trusted connections.

WHAT DO PEOPLE THINK YOU DO?

To gain insights into this, I encourage you to reach out to people you trust, especially those who you believe could refer potential business your way. If you are not getting needle moving introductions or opportunities, people do not understand what you do or what you want to do.

Remember, success in the ever-evolving world of sales requires adaptation. Upgrade your approach to reflect the changing landscape and the needs of your clients. Enhance your listening skills, ask meaningful questions, and tailor your message to resonate with your audience. By doing so, you'll stand out from the crowd and build stronger connections.

So, take charge of your sales journey, armed with a fresh perspective and an unwavering commitment to effective communication. Success awaits those who are willing to evolve and embrace the changing tides of the sales landscape.

BUILDING TRUST, CREATING OPPORTUNITIES, AND THE POWER OF NETWORKING

People work with people they know, like, and trust, which means you must focus energy on building meaningful relationships. How? Well, networking is usually the key to beginning business relationships and you need to start by recognizing the value you can bring to new relationships. It begins with being interested in the other person and asking questions to find points of commonality or situations where you can support them outside of the transaction. Questions like: "What's your greatest passion outside of work?", "Your special talent?", "Why do people enjoy working with you?"

For example, I'm a good connector because my business mission is that the work has to do more than affect the bottom line. It's not always about the transaction. It's the testimony. When you know what your "Why" is, and you can communicate it effectively, it makes people think, "this is a person I want to introduce to so-and-so."

Think about what makes you fun to be around. Why would I want to have a cup of coffee with you? I don't want to be sitting there with my hand on my wallet waiting for you to try to sell me something. And, keep in mind that not everyone is your ideal client, but that doesn't mean they don't know someone who is your ideal client. But in order to access their network, you need to bring something to the relationship.

When engaging in a coffee conversation with someone, my objective is to leave them thinking, "How can we work together?" or "I know someone you need to meet." That moment is something that is a difference maker when attending virtual meetings. It's crucial to leverage every single interaction to its fullest potential. However, let me emphasize that pitching and selling are not the objectives here. Focus on creating a connection that will make you memorable to the person you are engaging.

I've witnessed individuals being swiftly removed from platforms for bombarding chat rooms with lengthy dissertations about their company and its offerings. That's not what networking is about. Instead, it's an opportunity to learn more about each other, our motivations, and the results we provide. It is no time for how you do what you do. This mutual understanding builds trust, allowing us to confidently introduce one another to our trusted contacts. We want to be seen as individuals worthy of our connections' reputation. Every meeting should be leveraged effectively.

Rather than focusing on selling, shift your mindset to building meaningful connections. Take the time to listen actively and understand the needs and aspirations of others. Share your own story, passions, and expertise in a way that resonates with your audience.

By doing so, you establish yourself as someone who genuinely cares about their success and can be trusted with valuable introductions. To make the most of networking events, it's essential to evaluate whether the room contains individuals who represent your ideal client.

While it's natural to gravitate towards familiar faces or those within your industry, expanding your horizons and seeking out your target audience is crucial. Don't limit yourself to your comfort zone; instead, actively engage with those who align with your ideal client profile.

These are the individuals who are more likely to benefit from your services and potentially become long-term partners or clients. In my book, *You Lost Me @ Hello: Actionable Principles That Move You Beyond Networking*, I emphasize the importance of understanding the flow of networking events.

Consider whether the attendees represent your target audience. Look for individuals who can benefit from your expertise and solutions. Engage with them authentically, seeking to learn about their challenges and goals. By doing so, you'll be able to build stronger connections and identify potential opportunities for collaboration or referrals.

In conclusion, networking is not about a one-sided sales pitch. It's about establishing trust, building relationships, and creating opportunities for collaboration.

Leverage every meeting to its fullest by actively listening, sharing your story, and genuinely connecting with others. Remember, it's not about the quantity of connections but the quality of those connections. Seek out individuals who represent your ideal client and make a lasting impact through authentic engagement.

Networking should be enjoyable, a way to make new friends, new business acquaintances, new clients, and new connections in general. When you truly care about other people, it shows. When you combine this with your superpower, then all your networking efforts should produce positive results. Moving the conversation from "Pleased to meet you", to "Thank you for your business."

UNLOCKING THE POWER OF SALES: BREAKING THE GLASS CEILING

Throughout my journey as a sales professional and business coach, I have witnessed, firsthand, the transformative impact that understanding and applying sales principles can have on a woman's journey to breaking the glass ceiling. By leveraging the art of selling, women can amplify their voices, showcase their value, and create remarkable opportunities for themselves.

I want to share with you some inspiring stories of how I have utilized these principles and how my clients have excelled when they embraced my advice. One remarkable success story that comes to mind is that of a brilliant mechanical engineer who felt she was consistently overlooked for leadership opportunities within her firm. Together, we delved into her situation, analyzing the stakeholders involved and creating strategic sales conversations that aimed to make her contributions and capabilities better understood within the organization. By showcasing her value in a way that resonated with decision-makers, she began to gain recognition and influence.

The results were astounding. Within just six months of implementing these sales-driven approaches, she received a well-deserved promotion. And within a year, she confidently negotiated a new position, accompanied by an impressive 30% salary increase. But it didn't stop there. With a refined process and newfound confidence, she soon gained international visibility in her industry. This empowered her to take charge of her own career trajectory and shatter the limitations imposed by the glass ceiling.

Another powerful example emerged during one of the seminars I delivered to a group of women at a local church. As part of my free offering, we embarked on a "Make it rain" challenge—a call to action for each participant to monetize one of their skills or gifts, regardless of how humble it seemed. It was an exercise in realizing the untapped potential within each of us.

One participant, an exceptional baker, had a vision to create a non-profit organization. We worked together to repackage, re-price, and scale her hobby of baking cookies into a viable business.

Through strategic branding, targeted marketing efforts, and a focus on social impact, she transformed her passion into a thriving home-based and later a retail business. Today, she is not only satisfying the taste buds of her customers but as a successful coach, also changing lives on a grand scale through the programs she is able to deliver.

These stories highlight the undeniable truth that regardless of our professional backgrounds, we are all in the business of sales. Whether we're engineers, bakers, or entrepreneurs, most conversations we have in our personal and professional lives are, at their core, sales conversations. It's about effectively conveying our values, creating meaningful connections, and seizing opportunities.

Understanding the principles of sales and harnessing their power is a critical skill set for women looking to break the glass ceiling. By learning how to confidently articulate their worth, build strong relationships, and strategically position themselves, women can overcome barriers and unlock unprecedented opportunities for advancement.

So, my fellow trailblazers, embrace the power of sales in your journey. Cultivate the art of persuasion, negotiation, and effective communication. See every interaction as an opportunity to showcase your talents and contribute to your organization's success. Remember that you have the power to shape your own narrative, transcend limitations, and create the future you envision.

Together, let's rise above the glass ceiling and create a world where women's voices are heard, their contributions are celebrated, their potential knows no bounds, and they can go out into the professional world without any fear.

IN SUMMARY

We are constantly in a state of reinvention.

We must all find our own path and take the right steps to reach our full potential. When the facts and logic say things are not possible, know that with the right attitude, we are each capable of greatness in our own way.

Remember that regardless of who writes the check, you are in business for yourself, and every conversation has an objective.

Moving from a life of struggle to today, what I know to be true is that you must continuously examine your mindset—because with the right attitude...the facts don't matter.

DR. DONNA SMITH BELLINGER is a highly accomplished CEO and sales consultant with over 40 years of corporate leadership experience. As the CEO of DS Bellinger Consulting, LLC, she brings a wealth of knowledge and expertise to help her clients drive impressive results. Dr. Donna is renowned for her strategic approach and no-nonsense attitude, always striving to deliver tangible outcomes for her clients.

What sets Dr. Donna apart is her ability to engage with prospects in a relatable and humorous manner. She has an exceptional talent for "speaking their language," allowing her to establish strong connections and build rapport quickly. By simplifying the sales process, Donna empowers her clients to have more productive sales conversations, develop effective sales processes, and ultimately close more deals.

You are invited visit https://donnasmithbellinger.com/a-gift-from-donna/ to download her latest eBook.

To book Dr. Donna as a speaker or facilitator, visit :

https://www.askdsb.com/contact

Felecia Ward

Felecia Ward is a Fortune 100 Marketing Communications Strategist who helps amplify the brand authority of unheard voices and generate strategic visibility of servant and executive leadership. Her proprietary Strategic Leadership Visibility Framework™ combines the powerful fusion of bespoke personal branding, thought leadership marketing content, and media relations for C-Suite executives, dignitaries and celebrities.

The Importance of a Personal Brand

by Felecia Ward

Throughout my career, I was very fortunate to be mentored by wise females in executive leadership. They each had a unique management style and personal flair. I saw that they each exuded a personal brand that others spoke about when they were not in the room. I was also very fortunate growing up that my parents didn't assign gender-based roles to our tasks. Instead, they taught me about household operations and the importance of everyone contributing, which led me to develop a mindset focused on independence and business.

When I began my college career as a pre-law major, I had my sights set on a future in mergers and acquisitions. As a freshman, I was ambitious and eager to explore my interests, which led me to take on additional courses in language and English. Little did I know that this decision would alter my path and introduce me to a world I never expected to fall in love with. To my surprise, my visit to the Journalism Department proved to be a turning point. They enthusiastically presented a plethora of career paths in everything from advertising, public relations, and corporate communications to crisis management, and magazine writing. I was thrilled by the abundance of possibilities that lay ahead of me. It became clear that pursuing journalism could provide me with a diverse range of career opportunities, especially if I needed to start making money before venturing into law school.

Filled with curiosity, I enrolled in the College of Journalism at the University of Maryland, and from the moment I stepped into its halls, I knew I had made the right choice. The college boasted exceptional professors who emphasized the importance of internships, making them a mandatory requirement for graduation. During my junior year, my hard work led to an opportunity to secure an internship at Porter Novelli, a renowned advertising agency. A graduate professor who recognized my potential encouraged me to apply, even though I was still an undergraduate. Intrigued and excited, I journeyed to Washington, D.C., for the interview, filled with anticipation, and was awarded the internship. However, my excitement was dampened when I learned that I would be working in the market research department, rather than in the creative or marketing divisions as I had imagined. Initially, disappointment swept over me, as I questioned whether I was not good enough for those coveted departments.

Descending into the basement where the market research department was located, I later came to realize that this unexpected turn would forever change my life. I was introduced to the team of researchers who worked on global projects, traveling to countries like Ghana and Singapore to conduct in-depth cultural and marketing research. They shared their experiences, detailing their work in focus groups, studying history, and delving into the core of what makes a market tick. These researchers became my mentors, generously imparting their knowledge and emphasizing the crucial role market research played in all aspects of advertising and marketing.

At my next internship, I began to take on speech writing duties and I was given an incredible opportunity to submit my recommended speech for the CEO of Sunoco. Although there was no guarantee that he would use it, our department tradition involved submitting five speeches for his consideration. The CEO himself would ultimately review and select the one that resonated with him the most. I was determined to give it my best shot.

With those instructions in mind, I immersed myself in crafting the perfect speech. I poured my heart and soul into the words, carefully choosing each phrase to convey the CEO's vision and message. It was an exhilarating experience to be tasked with capturing the essence of a leader and delivering it to an eager audience.

When the time came, I submitted my speech, hopeful that it would make an impact. Soon after, I received an unexpected phone call. It was the CEO of Sunoco, informing me that he had chosen my speech as the best among the submissions. I was elated and overwhelmed with a sense of accomplishment. In that moment, I realized that I had officially become a speechwriter, earning the recognition and trust of a prominent CEO.

The thrill of seeing my words come to life as the CEO delivered the keynote speech was indescribable. I was just twenty years old at the time, and to have the opportunity to counsel a CEO and witness him delivering my words to a captivated audience was truly an addictive experience. The CEO even took the time to provide feedback on my speech, commending me for capturing his voice and delivering a message that resonated with him. This made all the hours I had spent watching his previous speeches, and meticulously analyzing his tone, messaging, and delivery worth it! It became clear to me that when writing for someone else, it was crucial to speak in their authentic voice.

My journey as a speechwriter and marketer had only just begun, but the experiences and lessons learned along the way had already left an indelible mark on my professional growth. I was eager to continue exploring new horizons, expanding my skills, and making a lasting impact through the power of words and communication. And, every step of the way, I found myself being mentored by exceptional women who wanted to see me succeed.

THE FIRST RUNG ON THE LADDER

Armed with the knowledge I acquired from my esteemed mentors and the valuable experiences gained through client interactions, I embarked on a thrilling journey that led me to my first job in an advertising agency as a junior account executive. Happily, this entry-level position would be the starting point of a remarkable ascent up the corporate ladder.

With unwavering determination and a hunger to excel, I worked diligently, gradually progressing from junior account executive to account executive, and eventually to the esteemed position of senior account executive. But my journey did not stop there. I continued to challenge myself and push beyond boundaries, ultimately achieving the remarkable milestone of becoming the Associate Vice President of Client Services.

Unlike some who are handed positions on a silver platter, I had to earn each promotion through sheer dedication and a proven track record of delivering exceptional results. I was entrusted with key accounts, initially working with Fortune 500 companies, and later collaborating on political campaigns, ranging from local elections to national dignitaries. I had the privilege of working alongside White House staff, government entities, lobbyists, and other corporate entities.

Amidst the dynamic world of public relations and corporate communications, the looming threat of crises is ever-present. It was during these high-pressure situations that I discovered my niche—an inherent affinity for reputation management. Whether it was mitigating the fallout from a violent incident or offering strategic counsel during a crisis, I found myself uniquely positioned to lend my expertise and guidance to C-level executives.

Differentiating myself in the marketplace and dominating my niche became my goals. I learned the importance of internal empowerment and not seeking external validation. Tragedies, such as job layoffs and the unexpected death of my mother, taught me valuable life lessons and the need to redirect my energies toward challenges and goals.

THE POWER OF MENTORSHIP

Mentorship continues to be an invaluable business and life resource. I encourage everyone to secure a mentor for each new phase of their life to build and grow, to learn and model best practices, and to learn insights not taught in books or classrooms. Seek wise counsel when you reach an impasse or there are too many forks in the road along your way.

Throughout my career, I have had many mentors who have made a profound impact on my mindset, my skillset, and my future. I will always remember one of my first mentors, who gave me sound advice as an intern. Her best bit of advice was to never make coffee! If someone asked, my response should be that I drank tea, and that I would TRY to make coffee. She then walked me to the administrative area to show me 10 women who had also thought to pursue careers in journalism and marketing, but they had made coffee, cleared out the fridge, and organized birthday cakes – which meant they were now trapped in administration as "working wives." She then went on to explain that men always "rescued" the male interns from admin, but no one saves the women. She inspired me to be the boss that would ask the female intern about her hopes and dreams and then help them get out of admin!

CREATING MY OWN BRAND

Throughout my career, I had relied on the prestige of the companies I worked for and the notable individuals I had the privilege to work with. But when faced with a layoff during my fourth job transition, I realized I needed to undergo a profound rebranding of myself. The new job market demanded more than just a list of employers and statistics. It sought to understand who I was as a person—a daunting and unfamiliar prospect.

I found myself competing with younger candidates who possessed superior technological prowess. I questioned how I could stand out amidst this sea of talent. It became clear that I needed to differentiate myself within the marketplace. That's when I embarked on a journey of self-discovery and reinvention, focusing on my personal origin story and how it shaped my passion for the industry.

Instead of solely highlighting my career path, I delved deeper into who I was as an individual. I realized that prospective employers wanted to know my mission, my vision, my beliefs, my values, and what made me unique. I needed to become more introspective and self-aware of what I brought to the table. It was crucial to articulate why I was doing what I was doing and who I truly wanted to help.

The journey of rebranding myself went beyond simply updating my resume or LinkedIn profile. It was a deep exploration of my skills, experiences, and core values. I started by crafting a compelling personal narrative that wove together my professional journey and my innate qualities. This origin story served as the foundation of my rebranding efforts, enabling me to present a cohesive and authentic image to potential employers.

Next, I identified my mission and vision—what I aimed to achieve in my career and how I envisioned making a difference. This clarity helped me align my goals and aspirations with the organizations I targeted. It also allowed me to articulate my unique selling proposition and value proposition, showcasing what set me apart from other candidates.

But rebranding myself was not just about the external image I projected; it also required internal reflection. I took the time to explore my passions, strengths, and areas for growth. By understanding my own motivations and desires, I could present a genuine and enthusiastic version of myself to employers.

As I navigated the job market armed with my new brand, I encountered a shift in the way I was perceived. Prospective employers responded positively to my personal story, my clear vision, and my genuine passion for marketing. I no longer felt like just another candidate with a laundry list of experiences; I had become a compelling and memorable individual with a unique story to tell.

Rebranding myself was not an easy process. It demanded introspection, self-assessment, and the courage to embrace my true identity. But the effort was worthwhile. It empowered me to confidently communicate my value, showcase my personal brand, and find alignment with organizations that appreciated my authentic self.

CREATING MY OWN LADDER

While still pursuing job offers, I continued to consult on the side, utilizing my expertise and knowledge to assist clients in their communications endeavors. The demand for my services remained steady, and as I weighed my options, I began to entertain the idea of transforming my consulting work into a full-time venture. It seemed like the natural progression—a path where I could channel my passion and skills into a venture that would not only bring fulfillment but also offer value to those seeking guidance.

That's when it struck me. I realized that my personal origin story, intertwined with my passion and values, held the key to setting myself apart. I delved into introspection, becoming more self-aware of what I truly brought to the table. I questioned my mission, my vision, my beliefs, my values, and my unique selling proposition. I recognized that I, as an individual, was my own brand—a distinct entity that needed a voice and a purpose. I decided to name my brand after myself, embracing my identity as Felecia Ward, the marketer. By incorporating my profession into my brand, I conveyed my expertise and specialization while also emphasizing my personal touch and passion for marketing.

In 2020, as the world grappled with the challenges posed by the pandemic, I took a leap of faith and officially licensed Felecia Ward Marketing. Since then, my business has experienced continuous growth and success. I have had the privilege of working with small business owners, executive leadership, and individuals aspiring to leadership roles. It is through these engagements that I discovered a significant gap in training and development for aspiring leaders.

Recognizing this void, I embraced the opportunity to collaborate with aspiring leaders, providing them with the guidance and support they need to flourish in their professional journeys. I firmly believe that training and development are essential for fostering the next generation of leaders. By working closely with these individuals, I help them define their messaging, establish their personal brands, and position themselves for leadership roles.

With the birth of Felecia Ward Marketing, I embarked on a new career trajectory—one rooted in authenticity, personal connection, and the pursuit of meaningful transformations. My focus shifted from simply chasing success to making a genuine difference in the lives of those I served. I had decided to enter the hallowed halls of servant leadership.

In today's competitive landscape, having a strong personal brand is vital. It is the key to unlocking new job opportunities and positioning oneself for success in leadership positions. I have witnessed firsthand the transformative power of building a brand, both for individuals and organizations. It goes beyond simply highlighting skills and experience; it involves crafting a compelling narrative that resonates with the target audience and sets one apart from the competition.

In an era of rapid change and evolving communication channels, I remain committed to staying at the forefront of industry trends and best practices. I understand the importance of adaptability and embracing new technologies to effectively reach target audiences. By harnessing the power of digital platforms, social media, and strategic communication strategies, I equip my clients with the tools they need to thrive in today's fast-paced business landscape.

As I continue to guide executives, aspiring leaders, and small business owners, I am fueled by the belief that everyone has a unique story to tell. By assisting them in defining their messaging and cultivating their personal brands, I empower them to stand out in a crowded marketplace and make a lasting impact.

The journey from corporate communications to becoming a trusted consultant and brand strategist has been nothing short of transformative. It has allowed me to tap into my passion for empowering others, helping them navigate the complexities of their professional journeys and unlock their full potential. I am humbled by the opportunity to make a meaningful difference in the lives of those I work with.

As I look to the future, I am excited about the possibilities that lie ahead. I am driven by the prospect of continuing to bridge the gap in training and development for aspiring leaders, equipping them with the skills, knowledge, and branding expertise necessary to achieve their goals. Together, we can shape a new generation of leaders who not only excel professionally but also make a positive impact on the world around them.

So, whether you are an executive seeking to refine your messaging and elevate your brand or an aspiring leader looking to define your path, I am here to guide and support you on your journey.

EMPOWERING HER PERSONAL BRAND: A CASE STUDY IN CAREER ADVANCEMENT

As a personal branding coach, I have had the privilege of working with numerous individuals seeking to elevate their professional trajectories. One particular case stands out—a top female executive in a prominent organization who had encountered significant obstacles on her journey to career advancement. Despite her exceptional competence and unwavering dedication, she was passed over for promotion not once, but twice, due to a lack of visibility and recognition within her workplace. Recognizing the need for a fresh approach, she sought my assistance in empowering her personal brand and reclaiming control over her career.

Our engagement objective was clear: to develop a unique and authentic personal brand identity for her that resonated with her personality and values. We also aimed to create a strategic plan to enhance her visibility, influence, and professional relationships within her industry and organization.

To kickstart the process, we began by crafting a compelling portfolio that showcased her achievements and capabilities. Utilizing an infographic format, we highlighted her skills, educational background, and notable projects. By incorporating quantifiable metrics and testimonials, we underscored the immense value she had delivered to her clients and employer throughout her career. The portfolio not only served as a visual representation of her accomplishments but also as a powerful tool for presenting her credentials with confidence and impact.

However, a strong portfolio alone was not enough to propel her forward. We needed to position her as a thought leader and establish her authority in her field. To achieve this, we designed a captivating speaker one-sheet featuring three engaging and relevant topics that she could present to diverse audiences. By strategically securing paid speaking opportunities at industry events, local business groups, and women's organizations, she had the platform to share her insights, showcase her expertise, and connect with key stakeholders.

The results of our collaboration were transformative, reshaping her professional trajectory and accelerating her career advancement. First and foremost, her increased visibility and recognition within her industry and organization were remarkable. Through thought leadership activities and speaking engagements, she successfully amplified her voice and expertise, resonating with audiences far and wide. Peers, leaders, and influencers alike began to take notice, leading to heightened attention and recognition for her contributions.

As her visibility grew, so did her confidence. The newfound recognition and validation she received bolstered her self-assurance and allowed her to break free from self-imposed limitations. Networking became second nature to her as she effortlessly built meaningful professional relationships. By engaging with key stakeholders, she expanded her professional network, establishing herself as a respected authority in her field.

The impact of her elevated personal brand soon became tangible in the form of career advancement and new opportunities. In recognition of her talents and the risk of losing her to competitors, her employer offered her a well-deserved promotion and a substantial salary increase. However, she made the courageous decision to depart the organization after a year, choosing instead to embark on a new career path in higher education—one that aligned more closely with her personal fulfillment and passion.

The transformation she experienced throughout this journey was truly awe-inspiring. From a professional who had been overlooked and undervalued, she emerged as a force to be reckoned with—a leader who had honed her personal brand and seized control of her career narrative. By leveraging her unique perspective and expertise, she not only attained recognition but also discovered a profound sense of purpose and fulfillment.

This case study serves as a testament to the immense power of personal branding in propelling individuals toward career advancement. By crafting an authentic brand identity, amplifying visibility, and strategically building relationships, professionals can shape their own destinies and create opportunities where they once seemed scarce. I am honored to have played a part in empowering this remarkable top female executive to reclaim her voice and forge a path to success on her own terms.

NAVIGATING A SUCCESSFUL CAREER TRANSITION THROUGH PERSONAL BRANDING

In the competitive landscape of today's business world, personal branding has become an indispensable tool for professionals looking to stand out and thrive. This truth was exemplified in the remarkable case of a male senior executive leader in a Fortune 100 finance firm who found himself forced into a position at a Fortune 500 financial investment firm due to a company merger. The transition brought with it a host of challenges, creating uncertainty and mistrust in an environment characterized by reorganization and a pressure-filled sales culture.

At the Fortune 100 company, this executive leader had implemented a gentlemen's company culture, fostered a systematic approach to teams, and prioritized ongoing professional development. However, upon joining the investment firm, he encountered a starkly different reality. Despite spearheading complex client projects and demonstrating his expertise, he received no recognition for his efforts over three consecutive years. The mounting frustration, anxiety, and uncertainty led him to seek advice from industry peers, who presented him with two options: fight back or resign.

Opting to stay and determined to secure his position during an economic downturn, the executive leader recognized the need to upskill and take proactive steps to elevate his profile and career prospects. It was at this critical juncture that he enlisted the help of a marketing communications strategist—the author of this article—to guide him through a comprehensive personal branding campaign.

Initially hesitant about becoming a high-profile commodity in a conservative industry, the executive leader soon realized the profound impact personal branding could have on his career trajectory. The strategist highlighted how personal branding had become essential in the modern job market and demonstrated the branding tactics used by successful C-suite executives. From leveraging social media platforms to creating impactful videos and developing a professional portfolio showcasing his top client work and agile project management skills, the executive leader embraced the power of personal branding.

Implementing the strategist's recommendations, the executive leader began attending key industry events, establishing associations with influential industry change agents, and volunteering at prominent charitable events. Little did he know that these efforts would pave the way for an unexpected turn of events. During this time, an HR recruiter from his former Fortune 100 employer approached him and extended an invitation to an exclusive industry event they were hosting. Viewing it as a nice gesture, he accepted the invitation, unaware of the surprises that awaited him.

Upon arriving at the event, he was escorted to a private room for a meeting with a departmental head. To his astonishment, the departmental head informed him that his former boss was planning to revamp the department and encouraged him to submit his resume and supporting documentation, leveraging the impressive personal branding he had cultivated.

The outcome of these personal branding efforts was nothing short of extraordinary. The executive leader made a triumphant comeback to the Fortune 100 company, regaining his previous position and securing a substantial pay increase. The transformation was not limited to his job title or salary but also extended to the work environment itself. In his new role, he now enjoys a supportive and collaborative atmosphere that aligns with his values and professional aspirations.

This case study serves as a powerful testament to the vital role personal branding plays in career advancement, particularly in competitive industries. The executive leader's success story demonstrates that by embracing modern branding tactics, such as leveraging industry events, strategic networking, and collaborations, professionals can elevate their profiles and open doors to remarkable opportunities.

Moreover, this case underscores the significance of ongoing professional development and adaptability in navigating organizational changes. The executive leader's commitment to upskilling and his ability to embrace personal branding allowed him to flourish in a challenging environment, ultimately leading him back to a position of success and fulfillment.

LOOKING TO THE FUTURE

As I continue to evolve in my career, my purpose remains steadfast—to help individuals and organizations define their unique stories, embrace transformation, and ultimately build impactful brands. I strive to assist executives in navigating their career paths, offering guidance and support as they transition in and out of leadership roles. Additionally, I am dedicated to bridging the gap in training and development for aspiring leaders, equipping them with the tools they need to thrive in an ever-changing business landscape.

My journey has taught me that the most profound transformations often arise from within. By embracing our authentic selves, understanding our origin stories, and aligning our missions with our values, we can unleash our full potential and make a meaningful impact on the world.

So, as I look back on my career trajectory, I am grateful for the opportunities that lay before me. The journey from uncertainty to self-discovery has been both challenging and exhilarating. I am proud to have transformed the fourth layoff into a catalyst for personal and professional growth.

As a CEO or C-suite executive, you have a unique opportunity to leverage your personal brand and thought leadership to grow your business, influence your industry, and inspire your audience. But to do that effectively, you need more than just a marketing communications strategist. You need someone who has a proprietary framework that guides the creation, integration, and execution of your personal brand and thought leadership marketing across multiple platforms.

You need someone who monitors the overall performance of your campaign and implements continuous improvement based on data and feedback. You need someone who can help you craft a compelling and consistent message that resonates with your target market and positions you as an authority in your field.

Today, as I continue to build my career and face new challenges, I am grateful for the opportunity to have rebranded myself. It taught me the importance of authenticity, self-awareness, and the power of personal identity. By embracing my personal brand, I have forged a path that aligns with my values and aspirations, and I am excited to see where this new journey takes me.

As I continue to evolve in my career, I am captivated by the ever-changing landscape of crisis management and reputation. Each day presents new challenges and opportunities to make a tangible impact on the trajectory of an organization. The dynamic nature of this field fuels my passion and drives me to continually expand my knowledge and skills.

I am grateful for the experiences that have shaped my career, from working with renowned clients to navigating crises of varying magnitudes. I am grateful for the amazing female mentors, especially the ones who warned me not to learn how to make coffee! These experiences have solidified my conviction that crisis management and personal branding is not only a profession but a calling—a calling to safeguard the reputation of organizations and guide executive leaders through challenging times.

If you wish to explore what developing a personal brand can do for you, then please schedule a time to chat with me.

https://portal.feleciawardmarketing.com/public/appointment-scheduler/5f77e09b2159217a9e407072/schedule

Melissa Stires

Melissa has traveled to over 33 countries to build relationships, seek investments, and design marquee events. She is a vibrant speaker, trainer, and executive coach. Through empathy and humor Melissa connects with audiences and clients from all backgrounds helping them excel in both business and in life.

Travels, Trials, & Triumphs

Why International Etiquette Matters

by Melissa Stires

When most people hear the phrase "business etiquette," I am sure their first impression is to wonder if they have fallen into an episode of a 1960's sitcom. However, the concept of business etiquette is alive and well in the 21st century, and it is of paramount importance when dealing with business on a global scale. While the term "etiquette" may sound stuffy and boring, I have learned over the years that it can be exciting and adventurous.

It was just before my senior year of high school when I left the country for the first time. It was the first of many service trips. Starting in Honduras and taking me all over Central and South America during my first few years of college, including Ecuador and Peru. Looking back at that young girl, a very humble me, from a small town in central Florida, if you would have told her that 20 years later, she would have led more than 60 delegations to over 33 countries around the world. I'm not sure if she would have believed you. But I did – and it was these extraordinary journeys that taught me everything I know about business etiquette!

VOLUNTEERING PROVIDES A LADDER TO SUCCESS

When I was just starting out in business, volunteering was the gateway to new worlds outside of my very confined existence, both culturally and geographically. These trips taught me the value of understanding the landscape of an area and its people. Those first few trips to Central and South America opened my eyes to the beauty of getting lost in language, foods and landscapes so different from what I had known growing up. It was those first few trips that showed me I wanted to work with people in these different cultures. This was not just something I wanted to experience once; it was something I desired to be a part of my world of work.

When I was 24 years old, I moved from Florida to Washington, D.C. for my first job out of college. I had the opportunity to be a volunteer at the Christmas Pageant of Peace, where the sitting U.S. President lights the national Christmas Tree. I always jumped at the chance to volunteer or be a part of events even outside of my forte. Being in a bigger city only widened the opportunities I had. My role in the Pageant was as a handler for American football player and actor Merlin Olson and his family. As Mr. Olson was playing the role of Santa I felt quite important to be his escort.

Those two days were so much fun and allowed me some of my first glimpses into secret service security, and how to handle a VIP. There were many famous people backstage and running around throughout the rehearsals and ceremony. I was in awe of all of them and each person could not have been kinder to me, including Mr. Olson, musicians Ricky Scaggs and CeCe Winans. My absolute favorite, my "Shero" if you will, Dr. Maya Angelou was also present, as she was performing a reading.

I knew how important this opportunity was, but it was hard to remain calm when it was my first time being around so many people of this magnitude. I was excited and a bit nervous and unsure how to interact or even if I should interact with the likes of the great Maya Angelou. But once the glamor wears off a little bit you realize that although famed and accomplished, they are just like everyone else. In my interaction with Dr. Angelou, I was able to have real human conversations with someone I had previously never dreamed of meeting. I shared that my mother was going to college after many years of raising children. I shared with her how thankful my mother and I both were for her voice and the power she gave to all women who read her work. I was just so very honored to meet her.

Unbeknownst to me, Maya had her assistant bring her a copy of her poem, Phenomenal Woman. She then asked me my mother's name and before I knew it, she was addressing the poem to my mother with a special message from her. I was able to frame the poem and give it to my mom that very Christmas. And to this day, my mom will tell you that Maya Angelou encouraged her on her college journey.

This small gesture on Maya's part left a profound impact on me. The great and famous Maya had no reason to go above and beyond for me. This was way before the days when stuff like this would hit the gram or be picked up on TikTok. She did this because she was kind and treated everyone with humanity. This was a lesson that I would hold tight to on my travels and my interactions with staff, interns, and leaders. No one is greater than the other, all deserve a smile, eye contact, and when you can, do things to bring joy to those that work around you.

I recall my team members being very surprised that not only did I have a relationship with my custodial staff, but knew their grandchildren's names and what they were studying in school. I remember celebrating one of the team's sons getting accepted into college. This man had sojourned to the US to build a better life for himself and his family. Celebrating this momentous win was something that came naturally to me. However, I realize that many leaders do not take the time to form these connections. However, if Maya Angelou can make a 24-year-old girl feel special, anyone can do it!

PUBLIC SPEAKING SKILLS ARE A MUST ON THE GLOBAL STAGE

I remember once upon a time hearing the saying that for many people the fear of public speaking is second only to the fear of death! I guess you could say I found this amusing, as from the age of two, I was singing, whether it was at church or downtown on the square or anywhere else I could find an opportunity to be in front of people, I took it. As I grew older, I began participating in debates and I won a big competition, beating out students from all over Florida. Performing and public speaking became something I was quite skilled at and incredibly passionate about.

I know many people struggle with the fear of speaking in public. Because I enjoy it so much, I also enjoy helping others to overcome their fear. I want to show people that they can be successful with confidence and the right tools. I had the confidence to connect to my audience, which was tremendously helpful in building an international career. When you know how to speak without fear, even if it is not in the native tongue of your audience, your strength and confidence still can shine through.

However, public speaking can potentially get you into trouble when you try it while heavily jet lagged! I was on a late-night flight from the United States over to London. We were there for a big trip we were going to be meeting with Winston Churchill's great-grandson, some local philanthropists, businessmen, and we had a big event we were attending at the culmination of the trip where then Prince Charles was going to be in attendance.

I was going through customs, and I was so tired and so jet-lagged, that when the customs officer asked me why are we here? What am I doing here? I was so honest and so delirious, I said, "Oh, I'm here to see Prince Charles." And that's all I said. Luckily, they didn't lock me in the funny room and interrogate me for four hours. But it does act as a good reminder to always be prepared even when you're talking to customs officers!

THE ART OF BUSINESS ETIQUETTE

While it may be tempting to assume that business customs are universal, the reality is that each country has its own unique set of rules and expectations. Failing to grasp these nuances can lead to misunderstandings, strained relationships, and missed opportunities. Something that may be a sign of respect in one country can be distasteful in another. Therefore, mastering business etiquette abroad has become an integral part of my travel routine.

One of the primary reasons why business etiquette holds such importance is its ability to foster trust and build strong professional relationships. Every country has its own cultural norms and values, which shape how business is conducted. By demonstrating respect for these customs, whether it be addressing individuals using the appropriate titles, observing specific protocols for greetings and introductions, or understanding the acceptable levels of formality in communication, you signal to your international counterparts that you value their culture and are invested in establishing a meaningful connection.

In many cultures, business is conducted not only in the boardroom but also over meals and social gatherings. Dining etiquette plays a vital role in these situations. Familiarizing oneself with the local customs surrounding meals, such as proper table manners, seating arrangements, and acceptable conversation topics, can make or break a business deal. Sharing a meal is an opportunity to forge personal connections, exchange ideas, and solidify partnerships.

Mastering business etiquette when traveling for business to other countries is of utmost importance. It demonstrates respect, fosters trust, and enhances professional relationships. Embracing the diversity of cultures and remaining open to learning allows us to forge meaningful connections and seize new opportunities in the global business landscape.

NEW KID ON THE BLOCK

In today's globalized world, conducting business across borders is increasingly common. To ensure successful interactions, it is essential to understand and respect the diverse cultural norms and business etiquette of different countries. However, I found myself essentially thrown into the "deep end" when I accepted a job at George Washington University in 2007.

The University recognized the value of international engagement and actively travels overseas to raise awareness and funds for its various initiatives. This strategic approach allowed the university to broaden its reach, forge global partnerships, and make a positive impact beyond its campus borders.

When I accepted the position of Director of Development Events at George Washington University, (GW) working with the then-president of Dr. Steven Knapp, I had no idea of the amazing future I was about to carve out for myself. My boss and mentor, Ms. Robyn Dickey had recruited me from a previous organization I had been a part of in D.C. I had never worked for her, but when the opportunity presented itself, I jumped. I would always volunteer to assist her on large-scale or small-scale projects, and this seemed to be an opportunity I could not refuse.

I was about to make a career change and she persuaded me to go to GW, where the newly appointed president was internationally minded. Robyn was a trained protocol officer, having been the first person to ever hold the title of Chief of Protocol for the United States Pentagon. She was an amazing teacher and trainer for what was to come in my career. Three months into my tenure at GW, the President, his wife, a small delegation, and I were thrown over to Asia. For the first time in my life, I was running events in the Republic of Korea, and the People's Republic of China. It was on-the-job training like no other. It was exciting, adventurous, and also incredibly stressful!

One of the first lessons that I learned was to be VERY specific with any instructions! I remember being greeted in Beijing by one of our hosts. He was very friendly, almost to the point where Americans might consider it aggressive. I was okay with that, and I was happy to meet him, his wife and his son. We greeted each other and he rode with us to the hotel. He indicated that he was a volunteer for the big event, and I shared with him that I had the name tags in my luggage. I told him that I would unpack my suitcase and bring the name tags down.

What I did NOT realize is that he considered this an invitation for him and his son to come up to my hotel room with me and watch me dig through my suitcase! So, imagine my embarrassment as I headed to my room with two unintended escorts in tow, who proceeded to stand and watch as I was unpacking undergarments and pajamas. I finally found the name tags, handed them over and realized that moving forward, I might need to be a bit more careful with what sounds like an invitation to follow versus being very specific with the phrase "I'll be right back."

While working and traveling in Asia, I truly began to understand the importance of politeness and manners. When you are in business meetings, people will agree, say yes, we can do that, and of course, that is possible, only to find out later that they were just being polite. These are common phrases used to save face, not to actually agree to a specific set of actions. It is also important to understand many Asian cultures feel it is very important to build relationships BEFORE making any agreements business or personal. It's very rare to have a 30-minute meeting and come to an agreement on a business deal. Many American businessmen will applaud directness and completing deals in a timely manner but in my experience working with people in certain countries that developing a good rapport and relationship should always come first.

THE LETTER OF THE LAW

Planning an event in Saudi Arabia instilled in me the notion of needing to consider culture when working with clients and others in business. It was the first time I had ever worked in the region, and I had a briefing with the Saudi representative in the United States prior to the trip. The woman I worked with was amazing and helped me navigate these new cultural norms. When I arrived in Saudi Arabia, I was working with a man who was my counterpart at the event venue where I was hosting my event. We had never spoken on the phone, as we did all of our correspondence through email. I was a woman, and I was his client and he was very kind and accommodating to me. These amazing experiences emboldened me but also allowed me to get a little too comfortable.

Things got a little bit different when I got on site for the job, and he saw a short, young, blond-haired woman, giving him directions and telling him what to do. I think it was a little bit jolting for him. In addition to that, the law of Saudi Arabia, the written law is that as a woman I needed to be modest, but there was no civil law that said my head had to be covered.

This was a major event, with attendees from the US diplomatic corps in Saudi Arabia, as well as many high-ranking Saudis. I was aware that when it came to Saudi citizens, men and women do not sit in the same room during an event. So, knowing that I had set up a separate room for the women. However, I had not scoped out the room and was not aware that there was a light well that had glass on the opposite side, which meant that both male and female service staff could see into the room. This meant that none of the women felt comfortable, and they had to stay there with their heads covered and were not relaxed the entire time. Even in my attempt to learn about the culture and their cultural norms there were aspects that I had not considered.

The next mishap could have been avoided if I had really understood that even though I was following the written law, I should have also followed the religious law. In that same trip, there was a delegation with five women and five men, and it was the first time that this event had ever been co-ed, with men and women both attending at the same time.

And I remember the religious police came driving up to me and the women I was with, (we had somehow gotten ahead of the men!) and they were yelling at us to cover our heads! Although we were technically following the written law, we did not have our heads covered and this was such a sensitive time as they were mixing genders at this event for the first time, ever. The religious police really expected our heads to be covered. So, it was a lesson learned. (And it was a faux pas that I will never make again!) These incidents seem comical now but mistakes like this can cost you in business.

A LITTLE KNOWLEDGE CAN BE DANGEROUS!

Most of my time traveling with this position was to places where English was not the primary language spoken. My President and boss at the time had a great ear for languages and could easily learn a phrase for saying "hello" in whatever language was required. However, we learned the hard way that it is imperative to ALWAYS have an interpreter handy for any exchanges beyond the initial "hello."

We were at one of the first events on our first trip to Korea when a short, older gentleman approached the President and present-ed his business card with two hands facing forward, which is the proper way to do it in Korea. The President decided to say hello in Korean and the gentleman spoke at length, obviously assuming that my President could speak Korean. However, knowing only the greeting phrase in the country's native tongue he did not know what to say and so, he just kind of stood there.

While I was standing right next to the President, the interpret-er was nowhere to be found. The older gentleman then repeated whatever he said and suddenly became very, very, very upset. Luckily, some other folks stepped in and explained what was hap-pening both to the gentleman and to us. The man who handed his business card so formally to my president was requesting his busi-ness card back in return. As I had just begun my journey into how other cultures work, I had not taken any official protocol courses.

It was situations like this that inspired me to become an official protocol officer so that I would be prepared for such situations!

Something to be very aware of when working overseas is body language and body interaction. As a Southern woman, it is hard to imagine a world where an interaction does not begin with a hug. In some cultures, and in some countries that could go over like a lead balloon and in other cultures and other countries they would take it a step further and add a kiss on each cheek. So, understanding personal space and body language prior to doing business is really important, as well as understanding rank and hierarchy of respect.

However, faux pas are not just for beginners! When I do trainings on business etiquette, one of the stories I like to share is about the G8 summit a few years back when President George W. Bush was the current US president. He had entered the room, greeted his male counterparts with a handshake and then went up to Chancellor Angela Merkel, the only female leader at the table for the G8 at this time and just rubbed her on the shoulders as a greeting. And I am sure that they had a very friendly relationship, as President Bush is a friendly, outgoing lovely gentleman and I am sure he did not mean anything personally by it. However, that moment was caught on videotape where the entire world saw one leader act in a way that was considered to be disrespectful of another leader.

THE INTERNATIONAL ART OF GIFT GIVING

Gift-giving has long been a cherished tradition in cultures around the world, serving as a way to express gratitude, foster relationships, and demonstrate respect. When it comes to international and diplomatic relations, the act of gift-giving takes on a whole new level of significance. It becomes a diplomatic tool that can shape perceptions, strengthen bonds, and facilitate meaningful exchanges between nations. Understanding the nuances of international and diplomatic gift-giving is crucial for successful diplomacy and building positive international relationships.

Another important factor in diplomatic gift-giving is the value and appropriateness of the gift. Diplomatic gifts are often chosen meticulously to reflect the stature and importance of the recipient. They should not be overly extravagant or lavish, as this can be perceived as an attempt to influence or create obligations. Instead, diplomatic gifts should be thoughtful, culturally relevant, and symbolize the positive aspects of the giver's country. This could include items that represent local craftsmanship, traditional arts, or products that are unique to the country's heritage.

Understanding the symbolism behind certain gifts can enhance diplomatic exchanges. By selecting gifts that reflect the giver's culture, symbolize shared values, and demonstrate thoughtfulness, diplomats can promote understanding and strengthen international ties. With each gift exchanged, a message of friendship and cooperation is conveyed, contributing to a world of harmonious diplomacy and mutual respect.

There is a video that you can pull up where then Secretary of State Hillary Clinton was giving a gift to the ambassador of Russia, and it was very formal. Hillary Clinton had given the ambassador a gift, a button, which represented a do over of sorts, to bring levity to the situation stating we are resetting our relationship fresh. Well, what the Russian writing said on the engravement wasn't what she intended. Instead, it said "overcharged." This is now an embarrassing moment that is forever preserved in time. So how we interact and how we do business matters.

WORKING WITH FAMOUS PEOPLE

When working with one of the richest men in the world you have a lot of expectations of what that will be like. You have expectations of who they are, how they treat people, and how they are going to carry themselves. Luckily, when I worked with Carlos Slim, who at the time was the richest man in the world, he was nothing but an absolute joy and delight, and working with him and getting to direct him in programming and events, and giving him awards was so much fun.

And one of my favorite times with him and his family was when he was given an honorary degree and all six of his children were in town and I was with them as we were running around from the hotel to the venue. Obviously, Carlos spoke English, but Spanish was his first language and so we were on the bus, and we were driving to the venue, and they started singing in Spanish and I joined in where I could. At the time he was the richest man in the world and here I was singing with him and his family.

Carlos had originally given me the nickname "sergeant" because I was running events and directing him where to go and as our relationship moved further along working together more, he labeled me the "general" because I was so just efficient and very direct. And I liked that because I wasn't afraid to tell him in a respectful way where he needed to be and what he needed to do and maybe that wasn't the case with everyone that he worked with. I still cherish it to this day that the richest man in the world gave me a nickname!

PROTOCOL VERSUS ETIQUETTE

Protocol includes internationally accepted codes of conduct and courtesies that are cross-cultural, written, and do not tend to change. Protocol is an important part of diplomatic practice linked with history, royalty, culture and language. Protocol provides an established standard of etiquette as you do business on the global, national, and regional landscapes. As the world's global marketplace continues to impact even the smallest of companies, business protocol has become a strategic asset which can set you apart from the competition.

I really did not think that as a kid from a small town in central Florida that one day I would be in the palace with the Queen of Jordan, or the future king of England, throwing an event for the Sultan of Oman or doing numerous other fantastic epic events and meetings with global leaders around the world. One of the most important things in my work in over 33 countries around the globe was understanding international protocol.

LOCAL KNOWLEDGE IS KEY

Something that I absolutely loved that we would do when we led delegations, if time permitted, we would do a cultural day prior to events and meetings. I think it is so important that when you are having meetings in Thailand that you can speak to seeing the world's largest laying Buddha or when you in in Beijing that you are able to talk about seeing the bell tower and walking through the Ancient Palaces. When you're in the Middle East and you're going to meet the Queen of Jordan, it is a great conversation starter to be able to say that you have swum in the Dead Sea, that you've hiked around the Wadi Rum and climbed Petra, that you understand the fruits and the foods and the culture and can reference that in in your meetings as just a point of understanding and awareness.

Just think about what you do when you host someone to your home, or you go and visit someone else. The conversation usually begins around comments to do with the loveliness of the home, or the tastiness of the food. You should always take this a step further when you're going into someone's city or country. That's part of who they are. That's a part of their home. So, when you can comment on the geography and customs of the place you are visiting, it says a lot about you and your dedication to establishing a long-term relationship. I drank a Caipirinha in Rio de Janeiro and I was able to describe how delicious it was. I loved being up high on the gondola and being able to look over and see not only the mountains but the ocean and the landscape where the topography was just so beautiful. Acknowledging things about a country makes people feel comfortable, and it makes them feel seen and appreciated. That is something that I always encourage when leading delegations overseas and doing business. I think the same can be said when working in the United States. We know that in the United States, doing business in New York can be quite different than doing business in Louisiana. Doing business in California is different than doing business in North Dakota. And if you put on the lens of trying to see the area and the space and the people and the culture and the food and you are observant and always complimentary, you are setting the landscape to build enduring business relationships.

DELIGHTING VS DAZZLING

When it comes to business etiquette and protocol, it can be a life-long process to learn everything about everyone! However, an important point that I want to leave with you is the importance of learning how to delight your audience, without going overboard and trying to dazzle them!

When you are dealing with the top 1% of the world's wealthiest businessmen and women, and the leading rulers of nations it's very easy to get caught up in the idea that we have to "razzle dazzle" them. However, it is important to keep in mind that these people have access to everything. And the idea that I'm going to be able to come up with a gift that is going to blow away the richest man in the world is a little bit daunting because he can pick up the phone and buy anything he wants at any time.

It really needs to be about doing your research and finding out what brings them joy, and what makes them feel appreciated. My first ever global forum was in Hong Kong and we had one of our speakers there who brought his whole family and it was a day and a half academic conference, where his eight-year-old son was going to have to find things to amuse himself.

At the end of the event was a big dinner, and I knew there was going to be the dance of the dragon and it would be a fun event. So, I made sure that even though the little boy who was up in his room having his own dinner, I told the guest speaker to be sure and invite his son down to watch the dance of the dragon. It was a small gesture on my part, but it created such a special moment for father and son. It was special for the father because not only was he able to watch his son delight in something culturally different and new and his son could now appreciate where his father had been all day and how important he was for the event.

A certain level of proper business etiquette and good manners is a must for anyone to be successful in the business world. In any social situation, there are things we're supposed to say and do, and ways we're supposed to behave. While important in all social interactions, these are critical to your business. Whether you follow these unwritten rules or not determines to a large extent how others perceive you and will determine how successful you are in business in other countries.

Cultural competency and international etiquette are essential to the everyday tourist, the up-and-coming businesswoman, and those who expect to be taken seriously on the global stage. Although the landscape is ever-changing, it is imperative that you set yourself up for success by understanding and implementing international etiquette.

If learning about international business protocol and etiquette would improve your professional future, then let's book a call and chat about it. The best way to reach me at

https://www.stiresconsulting.com/stiresconsultingscheduling

Mickey Quinn

Mickey brings her 30-years of experience in corporate retail of leading and developing exceptional teams to provide coaching, training, and consulting services to individuals, businesses, and their teams. Mickey specializes in improving communications, standardizing best practices in operations, and leadership team development.

Looking for the Leader Within

How to Be a Leader, Not Just a Manager

by Mickey Quinn

"It's not the position that makes the leader;
it's the leader that makes the position."
STANLEY HUFFTY

W hen I was enrolling in college, I met with my guidance counselor. When he asked what I wanted to major in, I said performing arts. He said, "How about we put you down as majoring in business and do the acting and singing as elective classes and extracurricular activities? That will give you a good base for a job in case the performing thing takes a while to generate an income." I said, "Okay!" And that is how I earned a Bachelor of Science degree in Business Administration.

When I graduated, I had no clue as to what I wanted to do. I had been working as a bank teller during the summers throughout college, so once I received my degree, I went to my branch manager and told her I wanted to become a manager. She said "Whoa, slow down there! You need to pay your dues first!" I thought that was what I had been doing by getting a degree. I was under the misconception that once you earned a bachelor's degree, opportunities and advanced positions just, well, appeared! That was my first of many rude awakenings to the realities of the business world.

Since I wasn't getting the warm fuzzies from my bank branch manager, I decided to quit that job. I then did what many people did in the mid 1980's, I went to the mall. At that time, regional indoor malls were THE place to be. I found a store, Brooks Fashion, with a "Now Hiring" sign, was interviewed, and received an offer for a part-time sales associate position. My retail career had begun.

Remote learning was just being introduced at that time. I was impressed with Brooks Fashion's in-store library of onboarding and training videos. My store manager sat me down in the crowded back room in front of a small television set connected to a VHS tape player. He instructed me to watch them all and then join him on the sales floor.

I had always been a straight A student. I thrived when given clear instructions on what to do and how to do it. Learning the standard operating procedures of a specialty apparel retailer was not much different than high school or college, and so I was in my element.

A few weeks into my new retail career, my store manager advised me that our district manager would be visiting our store, and he wanted to talk to me. The district manager arrived for his visit and asked me to join him out at the food court, which was, in effect, the office of all travelling district and regional managers in the retail industry. He asked me a few questions, which I knew the answers for because the topics were covered in the training videos. Next thing I knew, I was promoted to assistant store manager. Now this was what I was looking for! My boss tells me what to do, I do it well, I get rewarded. This was something I enjoyed!

In a few short weeks, I had landed my first promotion and my first title with the word "manager" in it. I was on my way. Unfortunately, the in-store library of training videos did not include anything on how to be a manager, let alone how to be an effective one, and it certainly did not include anything on the concept of how to be a leader.

Leader, manager, what's the difference? The difference is a big one. Both roles are involved with people, processes, and performance. A manager is responsible for the measurement of people, processes, and performance; while a leader is responsible for the development of people, processes, and performance.

I am forever grateful for the opportunity that Brooks Fashion gave me in my first management position, but it was during my tenure with JCPenney that I learned the most valuable lessons in how to be a leader. I joined JCPenney in the glory days of the department store industry. JCPenney was on a mission to be viewed as a true department store like Macy's, Dillard's, and Lord & Taylor. JCPenney mirrored many strategies that were being used in those department stores such as making cosmetics, fragrances, and jewelry main focal points, featuring a well-known designer such as Halston and creating a standardized management training program to train and develop entry-level management. It was in the JCPenney management training program that I learned about the importance of interpersonal relationships and the "soft skills" of being a leader.

THE 6 TOP QUALITIES OF A GREAT LEADER

Adding Value

When you help others succeed, they will do the same for you.

When I was a department merchandise manager with JCPenney, they used a "pull" rather than a "push" buying structure. The corporate buyers would put together a recommended product assortment, but the store department merchandise managers in each of the 1,200+ stores had the power to choose what product, and in what quantities, they would buy for their store. Each season, the department managers would meet at the district level to review the recommended product assortment and share opinions about projections. I would bring my department assistants to those meetings so they could learn first-hand about the new products and share their thoughts and opinions on what they felt would be bestsellers. This was not the standard practice used by all managers, but I felt it was important to give my assistants the opportunity. Based on their feedback, I learned how much it meant to them to be included in these meetings. They felt valued and appreciated.

I used this method of adding value throughout my career. When I attended meetings where I was not able to bring my assistants or team members, I always held a team meeting afterwards to share what I had learned. They appreciated my willingness to share my knowledge and information. They often had excellent questions and interesting points of view that helped me see things from their perspective.

A great leader challenges themselves to add value to others, especially to those who are their direct reports.

Being able to add value also applies to how you handle upline management. When you do more than what is expected, you will be noticed. Your extra effort should come from a genuine and sincere desire to help, to be of service. If not, your actions may be viewed as self-serving. If your intentions for going above and beyond are not genuine, you may come to resent those whom you report to if your efforts are not recognized and rewarded.

Working for someone you like and respect spurs you to do more. I have worked for many managers whom I have liked and respected, but the ones who went out of their way to add value to me made the biggest impact on my career.

When I first joined Coldwater Creek as the store manager of their flagship location in Sandpoint, Idaho, I reported to Skip Jones, the director of stores. I had never been a store manager before, but Skip believed in me. He personally showed me how to do the parts of my job I was unfamiliar with and even taught me aspects of his job. Then, he trusted me to perform. Under his guidance and trust, we increased the store's annual sales from $3 million to over $5 million, a 67% increase, in less than two years.

Skip was the one who taught me what exceptional customer service is and how to follow what was the JCPenney motto, "Customer service is our first priority." It was a nice statement, but it was only that ... a statement. Skip showed me how to take a motto and bring it to life. There is a big difference between having a motto and actually living it. Skip's expectations of how to deliver customer service were unlike anything I had ever encountered. He understood how adding value to every customer interaction would ultimately increase sales and build loyalty.

Look for ways you can surprise and delight your customers. Look for ways you can deliver more than is expected to your employees and your employer. When you add value to others, you add value to yourself.

Respect for Others

No one achieves greatness entirely on their own. Surround yourself with great people.

A common misconception is that when you become a manager, you are the expert, the one with all the answers. If you approach your job with this attitude, you will quickly alienate your direct reports, your peers, and co-workers. No one likes a "know-it-all."

One of the greatest leaders I ever worked with was Joe Gravitt, who joined Coldwater Creek as the vice president of stores when I was the director of store operations. I was not especially pleased. I had wanted his job, so I was disappointed upon his arrival and very skeptical that this guy from Foot Locker would be able to relate to our store personnel and customers. I quickly discovered I had a lot to learn from this man.

Joe had a unique way of building rapport with just about everyone he met—he asked questions. Joe took the time to learn about you as a person. He would ask questions and attentively listen to what you had to say. I know he didn't agree with everyone's opinions, choices, or lifestyles, but he always demonstrated respect. And the team in the retail stores LOVED him!

During the recession of 2008, Coldwater Creek's sales took a big hit. Our target customer was smack in the middle of the demographic that was hit the hardest by this challenging economic time. For the 12 months following that crash, our sales were below targets and raises and bonuses were non-existent yet turnover in our stores remained very low. Other retailers were still giving raises and bonuses, but our store associates did not jump to join them; the majority stayed with us. I attribute this to Joe's leadership. He focused on what was possible, searched for positive examples of small wins he would share with the store teams, and acknowledged that though our sales results were difficult, there was always something to learn and to celebrate.

That was a very challenging time for Coldwater Creek. We searched for cost savings, position consolidations, vendor changes, and headcount reductions. And then an idea began to surface that was way outside of the box—an introduction of a new brand, one targeting a slightly younger demographic of the 30 to 40-year-old woman, which was a significantly underserved age range in women's fashions at that time, seemed like just the innovative, bold approach that was needed to shake things up and save the company. But just as that project started to gain traction, the original founder decided to return to work from retirement, once again, for the second time, and take over as CEO and Chairman of the Board. The founder's return led to the dismissal of our current CEO and of Joe.

The founder had called me personally on the day he came back to work and made the personnel changes. He told me who my new boss would be. He had decided to promote one of our regional managers to the vice president of stores position. He then asked me to stay on, to help the incoming vice president to adjust to their new role, show them how the corporate office environment worked, and help them through the transition. I committed to staying on and doing whatever I could to help.

That may have been a strategic move to demonstrate to the store teams that "one of their own," someone who had worked their way up from working in one of our first stores opened was coming to the corporate office to lead them during these difficult times. Unfortunately, the incoming vice president had a very different leadership style than Joe. The incoming vice president was laser focused on the management of the measurement of people, processes, and performance, definitely not on the development of them.

I stayed true to my commitment to the founder. I stayed on for four years, doing my best from my position, to maintain the incredible culture which had flourished in the stores under Joe's leadership. But when leadership shifts away from focusing on possible solutions and instead uses a problem-centric approach, the resulting culture becomes uncomfortable and untenable. We started losing store associates, store managers, district managers, and regional managers. That is when I started looking too.

I received some great advice from one of my mentors as I was going through this tough time. He said, "Whatever you do, don't run away from something. You want to find an opportunity to run to." Very wise words. His guidance helped me hang on until I found my dream job as vice president of operations and customer service with a specialty women's retailer with 200 stores across the U.S., which then led to me to being promoted to president and CEO.

Honesty

The #1 quality looked for and admired in a great leader is honesty.

Honesty is truly the best policy. It seems like being honest should be a given, an expectation that everyone meets, but sadly, that is often not the case. In today's fast-paced world, opinions are frequently presented as facts, information is "selectively" shared, and knowledge is often held onto tightly as a coveted tool that the holder uses to wield power.

Throughout my decades of working in corporate America, I saw trends emerge when companies were going through good times and bad times.

When things were going well there were:

- Programs to encourage employee engagement;
- Regular communication forums throughout the company with all levels of positions;
- Town meetings where employees were encouraged to ask questions of the executives and board members;
- Genuine solicitation of employee feedback and ideas, and a process of review and follow-up; and
- An overall feeling of transparency.

When things were not going well there was:

- Discontinuation of any "unnecessary" employee programs;
- Communication forums became one-sided presentations, carefully crafted at senior levels with no question-and-answer sessions;
- Fewer company-wide and interdepartmental meetings; and
- An overall feeling of lack of trust and lack of transparency.

When times are tough, some managers withhold information. They wrongly subscribe to the belief that "No news is good news." Yet it is when times are tough that openness and transparency are needed the most. Sharing disappointing results with your team is of course challenging, but if framed in the right way, can bring about a wealth of solution-focused ideas that can turn a downward trend around.

Tapping into the team members who are on the front lines, dealing with customers, and doing the hands-on work is vitally important to the health of any organization. This practice has been used by the best and most successful leaders. No matter what position you hold, you can transform your career, team, business, and organization by seeking out feedback from all levels, and acting on it.

Another area where managers can find themselves tempted to be a little less than completely honest is in giving constructive feedback to employees on their work performance. Many managers dread the performance review process. I had one of those. At one company where I worked for several years, the deadline to conduct annual performance reviews was no later than March 10th, yet I frequently received my review from this manager in July.

If you are one of those managers who dread giving constructive feedback, here is a method to use that provides a framework for those conversations that make them much more effective.

Constructive Feedback: Give the GIFT of Feedback

GAP. Describe the performance gap: what they did, what they need to do to meet expectations of the job and why.

IDEAS. Ask for their ideas for meeting expected performance from this point forward and add your own.

FOLLOW-UP. Agree on follow-up steps and when you will meet again to review progress.

THANKS. Express your thanks, support, and confidence in them.

Being honest and transparent is so important in helping others feel safe. The unknown is often what causes us the most angst and worry. When you share good news, and the not so good news with your team, you create an environment where they feel appreciated and armed with the necessary information to do their job well.

I can't finish this section on the topic of honesty without sharing a personal story of how being honest impacted my career. I was director of store operations for Coldwater Creek in the early stages of their major retail store expansion. We had about 70 brick and mortar locations at this time. One of the team members from the technology team reached out to me to ask if it would be okay to take a particular server offline to do an upgrade. He wanted to do this during the day, on a Thursday. I didn't ask enough questions. I should have asked what systems would be impacted. I made the call all on my own, and when our phones in the retail operations department started lighting up during the upgrade, I realized I had made the wrong call.

The server this technician needed to take offline impacted our stores' timekeeping system. When it was offline, the store associates were unable to clock in or out. This meant that the store management teams would have to have employees track their time manually and then management would have to manually enter every punch into the system once the server was back up and running.

So, rather than telling the technician that this work would have to take place during non-store hours, which would be an inconvenience to him, I authorized him to inconvenience the stores instead. This was not an apples-to-apples trade off though. Having that server offline during business hours inconvenienced a few hundred employees, took management team members off the sales floor to do administrative work rather than being out front leading the sales team, created confusion, and frustration because the system was taken down with no advance notice.

When the calls started coming in, I realized my mistake. I owned it and confessed to my boss my error in judgement. Telling the truth, especially when it reveals your own error, can be difficult. It puts you into a place of vulnerability. Being a great leader does not mean you are mistake or error-free. Being a great leader means you are honest with yourself and others, you can accurately assess situations, take corrective action, and put appropriate processes in place to avoid making those same mistakes in the future.

Loyalty

> *"You don't earn loyalty in a day. You earn loyalty day by day."*
> JEFFREY GITOMER

Loyalty cannot be taken. You cannot demand loyalty. You can only earn it. The way to earn loyalty is to help others get what they want, and to do that, you must get to know them, and genuinely care about them.

After two years in the position as store manager with Coldwater Creek, I had to leave. My husband had taken a new job in another state, so we moved from Idaho to Kentucky. I became the director of merchandise for Wallace's College Bookstores, and then was a district manager with Barnes & Noble. I enjoyed both of those positions and my bosses, but neither elicited the same level of loyalty that I had felt for my prior manager, Skip.

When September 11th happened, my husband and I took a hard look at what we were doing with our careers and our life. We had two young children at that time and both of us had to travel for our jobs. We were living in a new town, with no established friends yet, and no family close by. We knew we needed to make a change where at least one of us did not travel for work.

My husband decided to purchase a small business back in Sandpoint, Idaho. I contacted my old boss, Skip, to let him know we were moving back and to ask if he might have a job for me. Skip immediately replied. The board had just approved a major expansion of retail stores. He needed me back now! Skip offered me a different role than I had before. This position was at the corporate office and would be more of a project manager and coordinator of cross-departmental communications. It was different than anything I had ever done, but again, he believed in me, and I trusted him.

Loyalty cannot be bought. No amount of money, bonuses, perks, or promises will motivate an employee who doesn't really want to be on the team.

Towards the end of my time at Coldwater Creek, I was working for that vice president who had been brought into the corporate office from the stores. They used the ineffective method of trying to buy loyalty. I received several generous gifts from this boss. Whether it was Christmas, my birthday, to thank me for the completion of a project, various events resulted in me receiving a gift, which of course, were nice. I appreciated the gifts, but I did not feel appreciated. The vice president's daily behavior towards me let me know I was viewed as a threat, not an asset. No matter how many gifts I was given, they could not cover up the fact that my boss was not loyal to me, and the feeling was mutual.

One of the biggest mistakes a manager can make is assigning blame to their team for underperformance and attributing themselves as responsible for successes and taking all the glory. A great leader does the exact opposite. A great leader accepts the responsibility for missed targets and poor performance. A great leader gives credit to their team when success is achieved.

When I was the department manager of women's sleepwear and lingerie at a JCPenney store, "liquid satin" was a new fabric being introduced. The first shipment of nightshirts I received sold out over a weekend. It was early fall, so I had time to get more product in for the peak holiday season. I did my calculations and confidently purchased 700 units. Well, I was successful in selling a good portion of that shipment, but the day after Christmas, I still had over 300 units hanging in the stockroom and more on the sales floor.

Our store manager treated the entire store team to an annual dinner after the holiday selling season. That year, the store manager came up with the idea of having each team of department associates roast their department manager. I was dreading the event. I was sure my team was going to roast me on my bad judgement of ordering too many liquid satin nightshirts. When it was my team's turn, they did a skit about how perfect I was: never a hair out of place, never a run in my pantyhose, always early to work, and often the last one to leave. I was stunned.

After the dinner, my team surrounded me, all of them smiling. I thanked them for their skit and told them I had expected them to roast me about the nightshirts. One of my leads said, "Mickey, you take such good care of us. There was no way we were going to share anything negative about you. We consider our team a family, and there are some things you just don't joke about!"

When you treat your team with respect and genuine interest and care, they will feel safe. When employees feel safe and appreciated, they tend to work harder, deliver better performance, and are less likely to leave.

Show your loyalty to your team, and they will in turn be loyal to you, their leader.

Success Record

"Confidence is contagious. So is lack of confidence."
VINCE LOMBARDI

How we remember important moments in our lives is an interesting thing. Our brains more easily remember events when we experienced strong emotions. I vividly remember showing my ninth-grade report card to my father. I had received A+'s in every class except for science, in which I had an A-. The only comment my father made was, "What happened in science?" The emotion I remember most about this event was one of failure, of having disappointed my father.

We often underestimate and underappreciate how many successes we have had compared to our failures. We are often our own toughest critic, especially those who desire to achieve more.

When I work with my clients on building their resume, preparing for a job interview, or getting ready to ask for a raise or promotion, I have them go through an exercise to recall their successes and achievements and I have them write it down. Studies have shown that the more you reflect on your past successes, the more confidence you will have in taking future risks. The more risks you take, the more chances you will have for success.

Professional Courage

> *"Real courage is being afraid but doing it anyway."*
> OPRAH WINFREY

When I first returned to Coldwater Creek working at the corporate office in the retail operations division, the senior vice president of sales and marketing asked me to check with the regional managers on how the latest seasonal floor-set was going. I called the west regional manager, and he said it was going well. He estimated that his stores were on average about 75% done, and after a full day of moving the price tickets and button packets, his region would be just about 100% complete.

I said, "Moving what?" He explained to me that after the last seasonal floor-set, the president of merchandise had been doing store visits and did not like how the merchandise looked on the sales-floor with the price tickets and plastic baggy of extra buttons hanging in the garment label in the center of the neck of all the tops and jackets. So, she had instructed the regional managers to have the stores manually move them to be positioned under the armpit on all tops and jackets.

At that time, Coldwater Creek's sales volume was vastly direct to consumer. Store sales were only beginning to register as what would eventually become a significant percentage of the company's business and eventually far exceed its direct business. All merchandise was packaged by the vendors ready to ship direct to consumer so it was individually folded and packaged in plastic bags. The process of unpacking every item to get it ready for the sales floor was already a more time-consuming process than what other retail companies had to deal with. Adding this extra step of moving the price ticket and button packet was causing even further delay in getting the new product out on the sales floor and causing an increase of labor expense spent on merchandising tasks rather than selling.

I went back to the senior vice president of sales and marketing with the status and asked if he was aware of the directive to "move the price tickets and button packets." He replied exactly as I had, "Move what?" Once I explained it and shared the calculation I had done on how much this was costing the company in labor hours, he asked me to advise the president of merchandise that the stores would not be doing this step anymore and why.

I was somewhat terrified to be assigned the task of telling the head of another department we would not be following a directive they had established. I knew it was the right thing to do. I was armed with the numbers of the added expense it was costing the company along with the number of days it was delaying new merchandise getting to the sales floor, but I was still afraid. I felt fear, and I did it anyway.

The conversation went well, even though my knees were knocking, I am sure my voice cracked. The president understood and even made a comment acknowledging that if our retail store sales continued to grow as they had been, we were going to have to figure out how to do a better job of working with the vendors to have our retail products sales floor ready.

Professional courage is being willing to say the tough stuff. It is speaking up when you know what you have to offer is the right thing to share, even though it may not be received well by others. Feel the fear, but act anyway.

BONUS TIPS

Believe In Yourself

One of the most important things you need to have as a leader is confidence. Having confidence in yourself is not about having a big ego. It is knowing your worth and believing in your skills, experience, and ability. If within the privacy of your own mind, you don't believe you can do something, your chances of success are slim to none.

It can be challenging to believe you can do something you have never done before. Your first thoughts often jump to how to do it. The question "how" is not a bad question, but when asked too early in the process, you may shut yourself down from even trying. Instead of asking "how," the best question to ask yourself early in the goal setting process is "what if?" What if you were able to achieve that goal? What would it mean to you, to your family, to your clients, to your business, to your community?

When you start thinking about what it would be like if you were able to achieve your goal, you start imagining that it is indeed possible. You move from impossible thinking to possible thinking. Once you start imagining that what you want is possible, then you can move onto identifying what steps you need to take to make it happen.

I have never liked the phrase "Fake it 'til you make it!" It always felt like a negative or a deceptive way to approach something. But waiting until you feel 100% ready to take on something new is not a good approach either.

Imagining or visualizing what it would be like to achieve your goal is a powerful tool that will give you motivation to take action. I much prefer the idea of acting as if. When you can visualize what your life would be like once you achieve your goal, you can start behaving as if you have already achieved it.

When I was a brand-new department manager at JCPenney, I was asked to go to the local middle school to speak at a career day. I just needed to go to the classroom and share what school subjects were most important to my type of career. After sharing that English and math were the most important classes that pertained to my career, the teacher asked me to share what the possible career path might be for me. I said, "to become CEO, to run the company." I remember a sixth-grade boy sitting in the front row of the classroom scoffed at me and said sarcastically, "Yeah, right!" My reply was, "Yes! Why not?"

I fully believed that I could become a CEO of a retail company. I believed in myself, and I believed I could learn what I needed in order to achieve that level. Decades later when my boss, the CEO at Vanity, told me he was leaving the company just one year after he had recruited me, I paused for a moment to process this information, and then I asked him, "Do I get your job?" He burst out laughing. I didn't take offense to his response. It was just his reaction in the moment to my unexpected question.

I left his office and went to my own office, and then he called me. He apologized for his response. He said that was not a reflection of my abilities, it just caught him off guard. The owner/chairman of Vanity flew into town later that day to discuss the succession plan with the exiting CEO. The following day, the owner/chairman asked me to step up into the role of President and CEO of the company.

Twenty-eight years had passed between the day that sixth grade boy challenged my belief in myself and being promoted to President/CEO. Our dreams and goals don't always come to fruition according to our timeline, but one thing is for sure, you will always achieve 100% of the goals you don't set for yourself.

Persistence

> *"Persistence and determination alone are omnipotent."*
> CALVIN COOLIDGE

The only failure is in quitting. So many people give up before they have fully explored their possibilities. If you give up, how do you know you haven't stopped one step before you achieved greatness?

Never, ever give up!

FINAL THOUGHTS

I have been very lucky throughout my career to have good mentors. I didn't have to seek them out. I stumbled across them just by being in the positions I held and at the companies where I worked. It wasn't until I left the corporate world that I had to find mentors on my own. As I was forming my own business, I quickly discovered there was a lot I didn't know, and even more so that I didn't know what I didn't know!

Whatever it is you want to do, whatever your dream, it is highly likely you will not be the first person who has done that. Chances are good that someone, somewhere, has already achieved what you want to achieve. Tap into their experience. Find out what failures they had and learn from them so you can avoid making the same mistakes.

I had always enjoyed the author John C. Maxwell. His books on developing your leadership skills have always been very helpful to me. I discovered he had formed a leadership development program that provided training and certification to become a speaker, trainer, and coach using his vast library of books. His program included an in-person conference where newly certified members came together with existing members to learn from John, his executive team leaders, and from each other. It was at this conference that John shared an idea that had never occurred to me. He talked about the importance of having a mentor, but he shared that you don't have to ever meet them to learn from them.

Another key takeaway from my studies with the John Maxwell team is to hire a coach. A coach is different than a mentor, trainer, or an expert who has lived the position/business/experience.

A coach helps you to find the answers within yourself. We often know what we want. We may even know what we need to do to achieve what we want. But the biggest gap in the world is the gap between knowing what to do and doing it. That's where a coach helps.

Tap into those who have gone before you to gain from their knowledge and experience. Set yourself up for success to achieve your dreams and goals by hiring a coach. It will be the best investment you will ever make because it is an investment in the leader, that is YOU.

If you want to create a compelling environment where employees are engaged and performing at their peak, or you want to give yourself a competitive edge by fine-tuning your strategy on career/business growth and development, schedule a time for us to chat!

https://mickeyquinnconsulting.com/contact-us

Kat Kennan

Kat Kennan is a certified trauma-informed and passionate marketing expert, known for high-impact, customer-driven strategies and campaigns for CEOs, non-profits, startups, as well as B2B and CPG clients. She specializes in trauma-informed and inclusive marketing services, using her Radical Customer Experience™ business model, an empathy-driven customer approach combining inclusive marketing, technology, and infrastructure to deepen brand loyalty based on my proprietary, research-based Radical Customer Experience Score. She is an active public speaker, advocate, and contributor at venues like SXSW, Vision Zero Cities, NYC DCAS, Forbes, ANA, RAINN Speakers Bureau, Serial Advisors, and iHeart Marketing.

Beyond the Mask

The Lessons I've Learned on Empathy In the Workplace

by Kat Kennan

ON MASKING THE TRUTH

L et's face it, we've all been there... the deep breath, the brave face, the *Oh, I'm Good*. We all do it when we get to the office (whether virtual or in-person). The idea that we should, and indeed must, be an alternate version of ourselves at work has been promulgated for generations. We all wear masks at different times and at different levels, with these layers demonstrating our complexity as humans.

However, there is more to these masks than pure human complexity. The idea that we must be an alternate version of ourselves at work has been a part of our society for generations. Women especially have fought hard to achieve professional roles — having to don a mask, button up and smile no matter what. I love this David Brooks quote he shared in a moving New York Times Op-Ed as Covid masking restrictions were lifted about the masks we wear all the time.

"Productivity is a mask. I'm too busy to see you.
Essentialism is a mask. I can make all sorts of assumptions

about you based on what racial or ethnic group you are in.
Self-doubt is a mask. I don't show you myself because I'm
afraid you won't like me. Distrust is a mask. I wall myself
in because I'm suspicious you'll hurt me."

–DAVID BROOKS

Masking is a source of self-protection for everyone. For women and other traditionally underrecognized groups, this has also been a common source of strength to cope with the various barriers, discrimination, and struggles we've faced and has become an ingrained behavior in our daily lives.

When we are expected to wear masks, there is a lot at play, well beyond self-preservation. We are told to "leave home at home" and "work life is work life," rendering the much-lauded work-life balance completely useless. For generations, we've been told that we must essentially have different selves for different areas of our life. The presumption that putting on a front, or a mask, in order to succeed is dangerous.

Let me tell you a story. I started my career in the IT industry as a receptionist during a time when managers giving undesired shoulder rubs and sexual commentary was both commonplace and accepted. I once had a manager who asked me whether or not my headboard was made of solid wood or metal bars. It took my naive twenty-something-year-old self several moments to understand why all the guys laughed. The manager was, in fact, asking me if I could be tied to the bed. Appalling. I went to HR about this, and was told to essentially suck it up. So I did, and my work mask grew pretty impervious, letting all sorts of harassing commentary slide right on past me.

Anecdotal evidence, however, has long held that this "keeping up of appearances" can take a toll on mental health. It certainly did on mine. Research also shows that there is a psychological cost in wearing a mask. According to a study published in the journal Social Science & Medicine, the suppression of one's true identity can lead to feelings of alienation, increased stress levels, and even physical pain. It was also right around this time that I experienced my first bout of what was then known as chronic fatigue.

Many of us end up engaging in behaviors that can be damaging to our work and personal relationships by pretending to be someone we are not, eventually creating a toxic environment that affects morale and productivity. We are supposed to be productive at work and contribute to company revenue, right? So it's pretty counterintuitive to expect employees to divide themselves in such a way. We must empower employees to express their true selves without fear, in order to create a safe and healthy workplace. As managers and teammates, we must make an effort to make work psychologically safe. Reaching some of these conclusions is what put me on the path to my current business.

ON CREATING A PSYCHOLOGICALLY SAFE WORKPLACE

Psychological safety is an attitude or atmosphere in which coworkers feel comfortable expressing their ideas and opinions without fear of judgment or negative consequences. Google did a famous study on psychological safety at work called Project Aristotle and found that this concept was critical to productivity and team communication.

There are two key elements about successful teams that the researchers observed. First, team members spoke in roughly the same proportion, and second, they were skilled at intuiting how others felt based on their tone of voice, their expressions and other nonverbal cues. Intuition is impossible to have when we are required to wear masks.

Let me tell you a story. Between 2014–2017, I started to realize how important this viewpoint was, well before I had any idea what it was called. I helped relaunch, rebrand, and reposition a 40+ year-old non-profit organization. As a part of the leadership team, it was my job to marry the direction the organization was moving with the ingrained ways of doing things.

As one of the first hires of new leadership, I met a lot of hostility and resistance. The entire organization understood the need to evolve, so I couldn't understand the resistance. And then it dawned on me... Having my voice heard was so important to who I was as a leader, but I'd forgotten how important it would be to my colleagues as well. I began having real conversations with my coworkers, especially the most resistant ones. I discovered that having empathy for their fear around change was critical. Their success for 40 years had been from the old way of doing things.

I've always been a stubborn person, so learning not only to listen, but to truly hear my colleagues was not an easy transition. I was easily annoyed and angered by their lack of cooperation, but right around this period (2015), I began exploring my own issues with impatience and anger through therapy.

I must emphasize how critical it is for leaders to be vulnerable with their coworkers and employees, just as I'm being vulnerable with you. For my entire life, I had wrapped myself in a protective bubble of intense self-control, self-deprecation, and anger in order to avoid dealing with the trauma of my childhood. On top of that bubble came all the masks I was required to wear.

For those of us who have experienced trauma, and particularly childhood trauma, our perspective on the world has forever been affected.

> *"Trauma shatters your most basic assumptions about the world— "Life is good," "I can trust others," "The future is likely to be good" — and replaces them with feelings like "The world is dangerous," "I can't win," "I can't trust other people..."*
>
> –MARK GOULSTON

This is an understanding that all leaders should have — traumatic experiences can make any employee leery to trust or communicate effectively at work. How many of you have had a bad work experience? How did you feel when dealing with a stressful experience at the new company?

I began to learn just how much my experiences were affecting my daily life by finally leaning into my past, which ultimately gave me a toolset to understand root emotions and not just surface ones. I used to lose patience, be irritable, and even lash out. I learned that my fear and anxiety were often expressed as anger, and that anger is always a secondary emotion. Something even more primal always lies beneath.

Opening up and actually speaking with coworkers, family, and friends when I was having a tough day and learning to be vulnerable made all the difference between a stalled organizational transformation and one where we were able to move forward together. We rebuilt our team dynamic and did a lot of great work together.

In contrast, let me tell you a story from my next employer. Towards the end of 2017, I joined the start-up world again for a rapidly growing food and beverage company. Company culture and values were a huge part of the company and were heavily promoted in the hiring process. Employees were regularly celebrated for demonstrating these corporate values in their work. The environment seemed very healthy with a thriving and communicative team, and I felt very valued and heard. The longer I was at the company, however, the more it became obvious that these values did not extend into the actual DNA of the company.

In late 2018, my personal life fell apart. I was suddenly living on my own for the first time in 15+ years, juggling shared parenting, and suffering from flashbacks, quiet panic attacks, and intense fear. My work suffered. I was in a vulnerable place emotionally, but continued to wear the mask of being okay.

I wasn't able to share what was happening to me. It must have been obvious that I wasn't doing well, but no one asked what was going on. As the second quarter rolled around, I was offered a generous severance package without anyone ever asking what was happening.

The multiple traumas I experienced are extreme, but traumatic experiences are incredibly common. In fact, nearly 75% of people have experienced trauma from a huge range of things. Every item on this list is a traumatic experience, and there are dozens of other examples.

- 9% have moved homes in the last year
- 14% divorce each year
- 40% know someone who died from COVID
- 32% experienced the loss of a family member or close friend
- 26% have a disability of some kind
- 10% experience a natural disaster each year
- 5% of children have lost one or both parents by age 16
- 25% live in conflict zones around the globe, including Ukraine and Syria
- 60% have some form of chronic disease
- 20% will experience mental illness in any given year
- 17% of women and 3% of men have been sexually assaulted
- 25% of women and 14% of men experience domestic violence

Your entire team, at all levels of seniority, must feel validated and safe. If this task seems daunting, here are a few strategies I regularly teach my clients, and ones you can start implementing.

1. **DON'T INTERRUPT:** When you interrupt someone who is speaking, remember that the message you're sending is *Your Viewpoint Doesn't Matter to Me.* No one wants to feel invalidated, so whether it takes raising your hand or passing some object

around that represents someone's turn to speak, make an effort to LISTEN WITHOUT INTERRUPTION.

2. SPEAK UP: If you don't understand something that is being discussed, ask for clarification. How many times have you left a meeting with a colleague and both of you had completely different takeaways? It is much better to ask for clarification, whether for you or for another team member's benefit. THE ONLY DUMB QUESTION IS THE ONE THAT ISN'T ASKED.

3. ANTICIPATE HOW YOUR MESSAGE MAY BE RECEIVED. This one covers a lot of territory, but if you are about to say something that is likely to cause a big reaction, consider how critical it is to share. Use inclusive language, avoid gender-specific language, and don't be inappropriate. A salty word here and there is likely okay, but if your message isn't going to be well received, KEEP IT TO YOURSELF.

4. USE DISCUSSION TO SOLVE CONFLICTS. We are never going to agree every time, but listen without the need to respond, and then take the time to ask your colleague questions for clarification. Sometimes the things that seem to be divergent viewpoints are actually more aligned than anyone realizes — we all express ideas differently. AGREEING TO DISAGREE can also be a valid strategy.

5. ENCOURAGE PARTICIPATION WITH YOUR TEAMMATES. We all have a role to play in making our respective companies successful. Some people, especially those more in junior roles, can be shy about sharing their thoughts and opinions or contributing to the project at hand. Mentorship doesn't have to be a formal process or program if you simply make an effort to encourage them. Be vocally thankful for their help and participation. WE ALL PLAY A PART IN THE LARGER WHOLE.

The result is a happier, more productive workplace, and employees that are more likely to drop their masks because they feel safe and valued. This leads to lower turnover and higher revenue. As

I've grown into my various leadership roles, I've made an effort to connect with team members of all levels, from interns to superiors. All my prior mentees have gone onto bigger and better roles, and I am very proud of all of them. You all know who you are, and I'm in awe of how you've all grown.

Staying quiet to listen better is something I'm always working on. I get excited by new ideas that they explode out of me. Remember, **psychological safety belongs everywhere.** I've implemented these same strategies at home, encouraging the voices and opinions of my kids (sometimes to my own detriment!). I never want anyone in my life to feel like they can't share something with me, and feeling safe goes a long way.

ON TALKING MORE ABOUT TRAUMA

When I describe what I do for a living, I speak a lot about the intersection between marketing, human resources, and DEI&B initiatives. While it's certainly a niche, I realized there was a need and opportunity when I was in the worst of my complex PTSD. I realized just how differently I perceived both marketing messages and workplace communication, so I created *Radical Customer Experience*™ in 2019 way before I was ready as well, and pitching the business was difficult. The year 2020 changed life in so many ways. With COVID, we saw both unimaginable losses, isolation, and the rise of Asian hate based on a misunderstanding of its origins. From the moment we all saw those horrific events on May 25th in real-time, George Floyd's death also brought forth a reckoning that had been on the precipice for far too long.

As I now sit here typing in 2023, the world is very different, and the need for Equity, Diversity, Inclusion, and Belonging. EDIB (sometimes referred to as DEI, DI, or DEI&B) has risen to the forefront of our collective conversation, even when those initiatives fall woefully short. Creating trauma-informed spaces is an important part of EDIB and recognizes the generational impact of what we've gone through as the human race.

The thing about trauma is that it sits at the root of *everything that makes us human*, our bodies, muscles and bones, and our very DNA. While I know this from my own experiences, I've also but I made an effort to educate myself about the groundbreaking work of psychiatrists, psychologists, researchers such as Bessel Van Der Kolk, Rachel Yehuda, and Brené Brown, and ultimately secured a certification in being a trauma-informed professional. And let's not forget the connection between trauma and physiological symptoms and conditions.

When I speak about generational trauma, I really mean it. Current research indicates that the roots of trauma go back as far as 14 generations and impact the following 14 generations. I want to take a moment to honor those actively working against the cycle of trauma because they are individually fighting against those past 14 generations and impacting the future for hundreds of years to come. Please do not make the mistake of underestimating the work of these survivors, of which I count myself as one.

So going back to the workplace, let me tell you a story. Just this past autumn, as I was finishing my tenure at my last company, I planned and coordinated a summit, nearly single-handedly (which is its own story!). During the day of the summit, a co-worker of mine was so focused on the content that he shushed an important partner of ours, someone who held a leadership position in a New York City agency. For my colleague, he was worried about the audience hearing the speaker. Of course, most people know that a good part of any conference are the discussions that happen outside of the formal panels. Exactly this kind of discussion was happening when the shushing happened. This particular partner had volunteered his staff to help during the day of running this conference at no cost.

He immediately expressed his anger and hurt feelings to me, threatening to immediately pull his whole staff. He vehemently said something to the effect of *"[t]his brings me back to my childhood, and my dad, and being told to be quiet, and oh no, this is unacceptable..."* As it happened, I was probably the person most perfectly positioned to talk him down. I immediately understood this to be a significant trauma reaction. Remember what I said before about anger being a secondary emotion? As I began to put out this fire, I was also impressed at his ability to articulate why he was triggered so much. It takes an extreme amount of self-work and empathy to understand these deep-rooted triggers, and yet he immediately expressed the connection to his childhood wounds. Most of us will only understand we've had a trauma reaction well after the incident, if at all, and we may never know the root cause.

Let me further explain it this way. How many of you have been in a meeting where someone suddenly has a meltdown? I know I probably have more times than I can count in my career. How did this outburst make you feel? Puzzled? Equally angry? Were you the last one to speak before this happened? If so, that probably made you all the more confused. The thing about these outbursts is that they very rarely have anything to do with the topic at hand. Most of the time, the discussion is that one last push to something that was already brewing for any multitude of reasons.

Let me tell you another story. I had a Lunchclub AI meeting recently where the person I was meeting with at first seemed to understand trauma perfectly, but as our discussion progressed, I immediately understood that was not the case. She felt such workplace reactions were completely unacceptable and shouldn't be tolerated. In other words, she believed that workplace mask-wearing was not only necessary but required. The reality is that we cannot control these reactions, and as we've already established the dangers of wearing masks, none of us should ever look down on a coworker who has experienced such a reaction. Instead, extreme empathy is necessary. **Remember how important it is to listen.**

In the modern workplace, especially in light of the events of the last several years, it is extremely important to accept a colleague's feelings, no matter what form, and make the effort to not only understand and empathize with them, but to make it acceptable for them to come back to the team without repercussions. Again, we aren't a *personal self* and a *work self*, instead, we are just these fragile, broken creatures bumping into one another. Considering all we have been through as a human race, especially in the last few years, this is incredibly beautiful and magical.

As leaders and aspiring leaders, we must encourage our businesses to make it acceptable to not wear a mask. If you lead with empathy, understanding, and vulnerability, your workplace will become more productive and happier, leading to lower turnover and ultimately, financial improvement as well. Surely even the most jaded or skeptical executive will support more efficiency and money.

When I first joined my last company in 2020, I started my employment while sitting next to my mom's hospice bed, her illness and ultimate death all coming within three unexpected weeks. Her death came on the heels of two back-to-back horrendously traumatic experiences, and a lifetime of dealing with childhood trauma. To say I was raw and emotional is such a gross understatement that I can't possibly illustrate it. The CEO that hired me, and whom I worked for directly, was one of the smartest and kindest people I've worked with in my career, and our working relationship was based around vulnerability and transparency (and I don't mean that in the obnoxious marketing sense).

A lot of the strength of our relationship, and one that was described by an agency partner of ours as the best working partnership she had ever witnessed in her career, was due to how I pushed myself to have the hard discussions and how open he was to having those conversations. What do I mean by this? There was an early team call where I felt unjustly called out by my boss for something I didn't think was at all my fault. I completely shut down and stopped communicating during this meeting (another trauma reaction!!). After I had some time to process our call, I asked him for time to speak to me individually. The phone conversation that followed was probably the most formative of our relationship. I expressed how blindsided I felt, and even more, that I felt psychologically unsafe during the meeting. At the time, he wasn't aware of what workplace psychological safety was, so I shared some of the research with him, including the Google case study I referenced at the beginning of this chapter.

As the months passed, I continued to be vulnerable, and we had many, many discussions of import, where I was able to share why trust was so difficult for me in situations in my personal and professional life alike. I'll be honest, I had some extreme reactions here and there during the time we worked together. After all, trauma can be a real mindfuck. But we always closed the loop on those fraught conversations and never left any upset too long. It is completely fine to take a day or two to gather your thoughts as both a manager or employee after a meltdown occurs, but I highly encourage you to have a follow-up conversation. These discussions are by no means easy, but they will make an extreme difference in the workplace in more ways than I can count.

Let's take a moment to talk about trauma reactions. We've all heard about fight or flight (or even more descriptively, fight, flight, freeze, or fawn). So far I've given examples of both fighting and freezing, but there are many less obvious trauma reactions that don't suddenly happen, but instead exist as a constant state. What do I mean by this? Are you a perfectionist? Are you harder on yourself than anyone else? I know many of you are responding yes right now. Perfectionism is a way trauma survivors can manifest their experiences. Next time you run across a co-worker who drives you crazy with their expectations or precision, remember this. Perfectionism allows us to control outcomes (or attempt to), and controlling outcomes is one thing someone who suffers from trauma or PTSD never had while they were having those experiences. (A note to any teachers who may be reading this—kids experiencing trauma aren't only the ones who cause disruptions or have bad concentration or poor grades. They can also be the kids with straight A's that do everything as perfectly as imaginable so keep that in mind.) Some other trauma reactions include:

- Hyperarousal/easily startled
- Procrastination

- Avoidance of people, places or situations
- Feeling on edge
- Automatic mistrust or negativity
- Anxiety, irritability, anger
- Headaches, stomachaches, chronic pain

Do you have a coworker who suffers from a chronic condition? Many of us do, but sometimes this is actually our body's way of expressing the trauma we've experienced. In fact, a 2020 study found that people suffering from trauma, in particular PTSD, are likely at an elevated risk of developing autoimmune diseases, such as rheumatoid arthritis, Sjogren's Syndrome, fibromyalgia, and many others. More than that, trauma actually changes the way our brain works, with every negative experience requiring a minimum of 10 counteractive positive experiences to overwrite that neural pathway. For those that develop complex PTSD, we fall into the category of being neurodiverse because our brains don't process information the same way as they did before trauma.

These results bolster an increasing array of proof demonstrating a correlation among PTSD, stress, and physical well-being. This doesn't mean you should assume your coworkers or employees have experienced something horrific or even if they have, that they would be capable of speaking about it, but incorporating this knowledge into your leadership practice is key.

Let me tell you another story. When I first transitioned to a marketing role, I was at an out-of-home experiential agency, and in addition to working on brand marketing, and occasionally being asked to consult on social media-related client projects, I also worked on a non-profit our CEO had founded and was running simultaneously to the agency. The organization was about children who had survived violence, as he had during his formative years. It takes a lot to work on an issue you have experienced yourself. But one way his childhood trauma expressed itself were rages at employees, me included. At the time, I was told to let it roll off my back and to have thick skin.

Part of my job was showrunning a marketing podcast. Right before a show featuring the head of sales for a prominent music discovery service, my boss went into a rage at me. He believed that only CEOs and CMOs should be featured as guests because those in sales roles would be overtly selling rather than discussing a campaign or strategy. Of course, I had done my research and knew that this particular guest was the brand spokesperson and the one quoted in every interview instead of the CEO or CMO. So, he was the right guest. Despite being screamed at, I refused to apologize. (I never said I wasn't stubborn!) What was the result? Six, yes six months went by before my boss spoke with me directly again. Trauma reactions can be extreme indeed.

Liz Ryan, noted keynote speaker and author of Reinvention Roadmap, Righteous Recruiting, and Red-Blooded HR recently put a poll together on LinkedIn that generated over 20,000 responses asking whether or not it was okay for a manager to ask an employee whether they were having personal problems. As important as it is to have empathy and understanding, you may not know if it's appropriate to ask a colleague about what's happening personally. This feeling is absolutely natural.

That said, phrasing something like "personal problems" isn't a trauma-informed approach because subtly or not, it puts all the onus on the individual (employee). Let's face it, life is infinitely more complex. I did agree with the spirit of "Yes," but I think this needs a lot of qualification before it can be implemented. It isn't so much about crossing an employer/employee line, but whether or not you are crossing someone's own boundary. It's not easy to be as vulnerable as I've encouraged, and we need to allow people to proceed at their own pace. This is exactly why my trauma-informed corporate work takes time for companies to implement.

The perfect follow-up to this poll was a quote I saw shared by another HR thought leader, Bill Marklein of Employee Humanity. I think the spirit of this is right on.

"No amount of pay is worth a toxic boss — or toxic culture.

Human-centric leadership is priceless — be the leader you would follow."
BILL MARKLEIN

No one deserves to work in a toxic environment, and I've certainly worked in my fair share of them. But it's easy to say "human-centric leadership" without really understanding what it means or having a truly psychologically safe or trauma-informed workplace. True human-centric leadership is empathy beyond what you might think, vulnerability, honesty, communication, and so much more. The complexities of a truly inclusive workplace are just that, and also ever evolving.

We humans are complicated, with generations of trauma and experiences in our DNA and bones (remember those 14 generations!), and are all brought together to this one place to make and market a product or service. It's not as simple as an open-door policy or being overly communicative. There is so much more here! This doesn't have to be overwhelming nor out of reach, as I saw with my own and my boss's effort at my last outside job.

By no means is it an easy process to become a trauma-informed organization—it is a huge commitment that goes through the entirety of a company, from making a culture shift and changing your policies, practices, and procedures. I've realized that this transition takes training of all your staff, particularly management and executive team to understand the impact of trauma and how this understanding needs to inform the restructuring needed. Being trauma-informed requires hard conversations, a new or different hiring and promotion process, and a different kind of management support from both a technical and adaptive perspective. Much like one training on sexual harassment or diversity won't change your company culture, one trauma-informed or psychological safety training won't do this either. Much like psychological safety, this is going to seem daunting, but with a clear framework, you can get there. Some things to keep in mind.

1. **LEADING & COMMUNICATING:** It's important to have leaders who are invested in making your organization trauma-informed. They should consistently communicate this message and have a dedicated team leading the change process. To make this more inclusive, you can use EDIB language.

2. **HIRING & ORIENTATION PRACTICES:** When hiring new employees, it's important to conduct interviews and orientation practices in a way that's sensitive to trauma. This will help create a safe and welcoming environment for everyone.

3. **TRAINING THE WORKFORCE:** To ensure that all employees are aware of trauma and how to respond to it, it's important to have a plan for ongoing trauma-informed education and training. This can be framed as part of your overall inclusion strategy.

4. **ESTABLISHING A SAFE ENVIRONMENT:** A safe environment is essential for everyone to feel comfortable and included. Take a look at your workplace culture and physical space to ensure that it's welcoming and inclusive.

5. **COLLABORATING WITH OTHERS:** It's important to work with partners and other systems to create trauma-informed networks, communities, and systems. This will help create a more supportive environment for everyone.

6. **REVIEWING POLICIES & PROCEDURES:** Take a close look at your policies, procedures, and protocols to ensure that they're inclusive and trauma-informed. This will help create a more welcoming and supportive environment for everyone.

7. **EVALUATING & MONITORING PROGRESS:** It's important to have mechanisms in place to evaluate and monitor your organizational change, as well as its impact on the organization and its outcomes. This will help ensure that you're on track to creating a more inclusive, trauma-informed organization.

The ability to have hard conversations manifests in so many different ways. We all saw and continue to deal with the mental health effects of the pandemic. In fact, thousands of studies found that the impact of social distancing, quarantine, and financial strains were associated risk factors with suicide and/or suicidal attempts during the pandemic. As the World Health Organization put it, the pandemic triggered a 25% increase in prevalence of anxiety and depression worldwide, with suicide ideation, attempts, and completions increasing somewhere around 10%. (Note: all of the studies that were conducted had slightly different methodology and time periods involved, so a solid, agreed-upon number isn't possible).

Again, let me tell you a story. When I speak about the ability to have hard discussions, I mean it in so many ways. In my last job, we had weekly team calls, and two things are of particular note here. One, as a leader, I made an effort to begin each meeting with something lighthearted or vulnerable. We were all struggling so much, as the above data indicated, and I knew establishing this kind of rapport was critical. The second thing to note here was something I mentioned in a moment of complete sadness and transparency.

Sometime in the late summer or early autumn of 2020, I learned a family friend, who I'll call D, had committed suicide. Instead of keeping this to myself or only discussing it outside of work, I brought it up on this team call. I thought if we were all struggling, then something like this needed to be said. I shared D's story and begged my coworkers to call the Suicide Hotline at 800-273-TALK or 988, or me, anytime, night or day, if they found themselves in a tough spot. There is nothing more important than making it known to your friends and colleagues that you are available to them when it's truly urgent in this way. The discussion that came from me sharing my story was emotional, and more than one colleague shared a story of losing someone to suicide. I think we all bonded in an unexpected way that day.

ON THE WAY FORWARD

As noted thought leader and *Start With Why* author Simon Sinek says more concisely and eloquently than I ever could, looking after those around you is the best quality you could have as a leader.

> *Leadership is not a rank or a position, it is a choice — a choice to look after the person to the left of us and the person to the right of us."*
> SIMON SINEK

This means leading with empathy and always keeping equity, diversity, inclusion, and belonging at the heart of everything you do. This isn't an easy journey, and it will challenge you to rethink the norm constantly. Companies and leaders who have been on the forefront of things like corporate social responsibility, sustainability, and standing up for what they believe in are more likely to be open to adopting these principles, but it's attainable for everyone. It may take therapy, a business coach, or a consultant like me to help you, but it's one that is desperately needed. It took me a long time to get here, and I know this is exactly where I belong and what I'm meant to help people and companies achieve.

To learn more about how to implement trauma-informed and strengths-based solutions at your company, please contact Kat at:

https://calendly.com/kat-k

Barbara Alexander

Barbara is an intuitive coach, speaker and astrologer. After leaving a 25-year corporate career, she followed her passion to make a greater impact for women in leadership. Her unique approach helps corporate leaders and entrepreneurs reach their highest potential through leveraging their personal astrology.

How to Make Your Glass Ceiling Your Glass Floor

Connecting to the Cosmos to Reach Your Next Level of Success

by Barbara Alexander

ASTROLOGY IS MORE THAN YOUR HOROSCOPE AND SUN SIGN

When I left my corporate career over a decade ago, I had an inner knowing that I was meant to contribute to the world beyond what I had already accomplished. I didn't know what my calling was, but I had blind faith that I would figure it out! I embarked on my entrepreneurial path, and decided to go into the coaching profession.

For the next several years, I worked with clients across many different life, leadership, and business challenges in search of my passion and purpose. I hired coaches and enrolled in programs to help me hone in on my coaching "niche." I knew all my experience, skills, and talents could be put to use to make a greater impact. I decided to put the focus on my prior success in sales coaching and training, which was an area I excelled in.

This work was fulfilling, but it didn't excite me. While I had a proven track record for helping Fortune 500 companies generate billions of dollars, I no longer had the drive, passion, and motivation for the work. I was searching for answers on my purpose and passion that no other coach or business program could help me find. What I didn't know at the time was that the answers were all within me.

Those answers began to reveal themselves in 2020 when I met an astrologer named Susan, who was a guest speaker in one of my women in business groups. Susan was doing an astrology reading for another member of the group while we observed. She described the member based on the characteristics of the different planets that were in her birth chart. She explained that that the combination of all the planets provides a picture of her own unique personality.

During the reading, Susan talked about events that were currently taking place with her. She mentioned that there might be a change in her home and career or a job move. The member validated everything that Susan said. How could she know?

I was so intrigued that I immediately booked my own reading.

All I knew about astrology up to this point was that Cancer was my zodiac sign and I could relate to some of those characteristics. I read my horoscope as a source of entertainment to help me find out how my day might turn out–much like we look to the weather forecast.

I couldn't wait to learn more! During the reading, Susan told me that Cancer is my Sun sign, which is my personality, described as nurturing, caring, and motherly. And Scorpio, which is my Rising sign, is how other people see me: passionate, independent, and brave. It was helpful to know the characteristics that people see in me! Susan also described each of the different planets and where they were in my chart. That told me the story of who I am and how I show up in the world: what I need to emotionally fulfill me, how I communicate, how I attract love and money, and how I take action, to name a few. She also described some of the different relationships between planets in my birth chart that indicated hidden talents. Others, considered more challenging traits, behaviors, or patterns, were "blind spots."

During the reading, Susan also had this uncanny understanding of current and past events in my life. How could she know? I had never spoken to her before, but she knew I was having challenges in my marriage. I confirmed we were in divorce mediation. Looking ahead, she shared an optimistic outlook that I would successfully get through this difficult time in my life, both emotionally and financially. I held on to this hope over the next year, knowing we would be all be all right as the divorce became final.

She described my relationship with my sister, my parents and my childhood, and other family dynamics with my children. Susan told me that I was about to go through a major transformation period that would last several years. All of this information was gleaned through the skill of an astrologer looking at a combination of data points in my birth chart in connection with the current energies of the cosmos.

The vision for my professional life began to unfold. I gained greater clarity on my gifts and talents, and a deeper strength and confidence in my capabilities. I learned more about who I was as a person, and I opened myself up to the world of possibilities that were available to me. She pointed out that my talents could be best expressed and would have the greatest influence in the public eye, and I was inspired to share my ideas through speaking and publishing. I had always been comfortable speaking, but my vision expanded to reaching a larger audience as well as considering writing a book.

The combination of other elements in my birth chart confirmed that coaching and mentoring were a natural path for me. She even helped me get specific with the area of coaching that would best suit me. One-to-one relationships, personal and business, would also be where I'd find the greatest joy, happiness, and prosperity based on where several significant life purpose indicators were in my chart.

My initial curiosity to get a reading turned into an insatiable appetite to learn more about how astrology works.

I learned that my birth chart is a map, or an energetic blueprint, of where the planets were at the exact moment I was born. The information in my chart revealed my unique personality characteristics and my greatest potential, which, up until this point, had been untapped. It shined a light on where I had challenges and blind spots. Parts of who I am, which I had never understood or even seen before, were illuminated.

Your birth chart contains powerful information about the types of energies you were exposed to at the exact moment of your birth. When current planetary energies are "activated" in your birth chart in the present time, certain events and themes will play out.

How does this really work? It's energy. Everything is a part of a single, total field of energy known as the Universal Law of Oneness (the first of the 12 Universal Laws). You, and everything you experience, are part of the same, whole, complete system, and there is nothing apart from that energy. The basic principle of astrology refers to "as above, so below"–meaning, the planets in our solar system have the ability to mirror what is happening here on earth, almost like they shine their influences on the earth to create certain energetic force fields.

It was through my first reading that astrology became my compass, and my birth chart was my blueprint. Although I could not change my blueprint, I could consciously choose how I wanted to work with the energies in the cosmos. I had the foresight to know events would shift, and I felt empowered to co-create my own destiny. This clarity was incredibly validating and provided a new-found sense of empowerment.

My first astrology reading was an incredible life-affirming and life-altering event. I began to learn more about the application of astrology. It was another tool for my personal growth as well as my path to purpose and fulfillment. My birth chart laid out the path that would lead to my overall success in life as I become more aligned to my internal blueprint.

Susan and I met for astrology sessions every three months so that I could learn how to better work with the energies of the cosmos rather than unknowingly resist them. This knowledge allowed me to better anticipate challenges as well as to leverage opportunities for growth and expansion, both personally and professionally.

During one of our "looking ahead" sessions, Susan told me that I was in the beginning of a two-year cosmic cycle in my birth chart, and I needed to put greater focus and attention on my home and family matters. With that knowledge, I didn't feel regretful or guilty for spending less time on my business. She also pointed out that, on a personal level, it would be a great time to capitalize on the energies in the health area of my birth chart. I started a new nutrition and fitness routine, which looking back, helped me get into the best shape of my life since my twenties!

As my family dynamics shifted, the time was ripe to redirect my energies, in alignment with the current cosmic energies, toward my business. I gained greater clarity on the direction I wanted to go as I continued to gather more evidence of how astrology was changing my life and my business. Looking ahead at the cosmos, I refined my business plan and made strategic investments timed to the beginning of a moon cycle in the money areas of my chart.

One of those decisions came only six months after my first reading. I decided to enroll in a business astrology certification program. While my first session helped me unlock the hidden potential uncovered in my birth chart, I began learning how to co-create outcomes in my life and business by leveraging the energies of the cosmos at the right time. This inspired me to want to teach and coach my clients to do the same.

FROM CAVEMEN TO WALL STREET FINANCIERS

As I began to shift my coaching practice, with greater visibility of the use of astrology as a tool with clients, there were people in my life who were wondering if I had gone "woo woo." A relative actually asked if I did palm readings! You, too, may be thinking that astrology is "woo woo." It's certainly understandable as most of us have trouble believing in something that cannot be seen or measured.

But if you go back in time, astrology has played a practical role throughout history in the evolution of human culture. Mankind relied on the sun, the moon, and the stars for survival due to the uncertainty brought on by nature's cycles. The stars and the seven visible planets closest to the earth were the first GPS.

Astrology also plays a role in predicting financial trends dating back to the late 1800s. Pioneers of financial astrology emerged when the U.S. stock market was gaining popularity. W.D. Gann was a market forecaster who applied astrological techniques to predict future price movement in the stock or commodity markets. His techniques remain in widespread use among traders today. JP Morgan, who was the first to become a billionaire, was widely known for using astrology to influence his decisions.

Our familiarity with astrology has been most resonant as a source of entertainment. In the 1920s, newspapers and magazines began publishing Sun-sign-based horoscopes. The advancement of technology made it faster and easier for astrologers to cast birth charts.

As an industry that was already on the rise, astrology accelerated in 2020 due to the confusion and uncertain conditions brought on by the pandemic. According to data from Sensor Tower, reported by Business Insider, revenue for astrology apps grew to nearly $40 million in 2019. The industry as a whole is worth $2.2 billion.

IT WAS WRITTEN IN THE STARS—REACHING YOUR HIGHEST POTENTIAL WITH CONFIDENCE, CLARITY, AND COURAGE

As I began introducing astrology to clients through online classes and podcasts, many had no prior knowledge or understanding of it. They booked sessions with me out of curiosity, and to learn more about themselves. When asked if they had a birth chart reading before, they'd say, "No, but I know I'm a Taurus."

Some of them have taken assessment tools, such as EQ-i 2.0 (emotional intelligence) and Gallup's Clifton Strengths, as part of their professional development. As an EQ-I 2.0 Certified Practitioner, I'm very familiar with the inputs, scoring methodologies, and output reporting. These tools evaluate the individual within the context of specific skill sets and serve immense value.

I encourage people to learn as much as they can about themselves. Self-awareness is a gift that provides insights, and we get to choose how to work with those insights to become a better version of ourselves. Your birth chart is one of the tools. Every birth chart is unique and provides a holistic view of your uniqueness. When you have a reading with a professional astrologer, you will learn about who you are as a person, how others see you, gain immense clarity on your gifts and talents, and have greater understanding of what you are capable of.

While there are various ways to learn about your birth chart online, the insights and wisdom you receive when you meet with an astrologer are priceless. They can connect the dots and put the pieces of the puzzle together that system-generated reports and online apps cannot. Many astrologers view the client as an integral part of how the information is contextualized, based on their life circumstances.

To illustrate the robustness of this data, let's take look at an excerpt from a birth chart reading I had with one of my clients, Sheila, a leader in a major pharmaceutical company. She is also building her own coaching practice. She experienced several life changes over the past year, and she was looking for insights into her career and how to move forward in her coaching practice while working her full-time job.

Based on a combination of factors in her birth chart, Sheila learned more about her strengths and style of communication in her career and public life, her ambitions and aspirations. When it comes to her professional life, her birth chart indicated she was smart, and others quickly notice this. She has the ability to advance rapidly, and ascend to a position of power.

Sheila also discovered that she's skilled at communicating her ideas and tailoring the messages to everyone's individual needs. She doesn't just communicate; she communicates extremely effectively. She has a talent for transmitting information through teaching and sharing ideas. She has excellent rhetorical skills. Her skills are on par with professional public speakers, politicians, and teachers.

Sheila also values education, but more as a necessary step towards her dream career than for the sake of learning. There is a practical approach here: knowledge gained is power only if you apply it.

Sheila related to many of these qualities, which further infused more confidence in her regarding her public speaking abilities. It's a gift meant for her to share as part of her overall blueprint for success. She's now offering workshops through her coaching business to teach others how to overcome their fear of speaking and to become better public speakers. She seized this opportunity, as it came during a once-in-a-12-year-cycle in the cosmos that would bring her more abundance, luck, and prosperity in her career and public life.

An astrological birth chart goes deeper into the psyche of an individual. Many women come to me for a reading because they are feeling one or more of the following:

- Unfulfilled
- Unaccepted
- Misunderstood
- Unloved
- Unseen
- Unheard

This was the case with Anna, a leader in a large medical practice, who found herself repeatedly in relationships which provoked additional wounding. She had a fear of rejection, and no matter how much she did for her partner, she never felt it was enough. She also related experiences feeling rejected in the workplace–as if she was never accepted for who she was and her co-workers "were out to get her."

As with Anna's reading, I've always been able to find the hidden gems that show up in someone's chart that correlate to subconscious, self-sabotaging patterns. I showed her where there were energetic conflicts between two planets that caused this friction, which was spot on to what she was experiencing. Anna's reading was an epiphany of self-discovery, self-awareness, and self-acceptance. I often hear clients say, "So, there isn't anything wrong with me?" I am able to normalize what they have experienced and provide key take-aways for their healing.

Anna's feedback to me after our session was a true testament to the work I have been called to do. She shared with me, "During our session, I felt loved and supported with such brilliant wisdom. My session was mind-blowing in countless ways, and I know I'll continue to grow because of your talent and insight. You are a GIFT."

While there are so many hidden gems in a birth chart, one of the biggest treasures is learning about your North Node. It symbolizes the direction you were meant to move toward to accomplish and live a joyful, fulfilled, balanced life. This goes beyond your career and incorporates into all areas of life as one's Life Purpose. You may have heard the term "follow your North Star." This is your North Node.

Many women come to me with one or more of the following:

- Feeling restless and sense there is something more to do in this life, as in making a greater impact in career, relationships and community.

- Reaching high levels of success and recognition yet they feel something is missing and keeping them from fully enjoying life.

- Focusing so much on external achievement at work and at home and wanting to seek ways to feel internal fulfillment and satisfaction.

- Struggling with finding the balance between a demanding career, the responsibilities of a family, and their own personal sense of fulfillment.

- Feeling a level of uncertainty in their path having operated from other's (or society's) expectations of them.

Many of the answers come when looking at the conflicting balance between the North Node and South Node in a birth chart. With the North Node, you are often facing the unknown and an uncomfortable growth path; and with the South Node, you rely on your existing talents and stay safe within your comfort zone. As a coach, I can cut right to the chase on the work that needs to be done to align them on their true path to purpose and success. This requires helping them to develop their North Node attributes while leveraging, or sometimes letting go of, their South Node tendencies.

Kim, a successful CEO of a coaching and consulting firm, came to me for a reading when she was feeling an intense push/pull energy between where she wanted to make changes in her personal and professional life, and where she was feeling safe and comfortable. In one glance at her birth chart, I knew she was experiencing a significant cosmic event which happens on an individual level every 18½ years.

This event is one of several different energetic forces in the cosmos that occur at specific times in our life, which are meant to help us on our path to growth, purpose, and fulfillment. We both agreed it was no coincidence we met when we did because, with this knowledge, she knew what to expect. Kim had had a birth chart reading before, so she had a sense of how her personal astrology could help, but had never fully understood or embraced it. She shared with me, "You have a way of taking the confusing aspects (all the astrological words) and breaking them down into ideas I can connect with."

During this cosmic event over an 18-month timeframe, there would be periods of opportunity, emotional changes, and life changes, which would be one of the most successful and challenging times of Kim's life.

Kim's greatest challenge was moving toward the creative expression of her authentic self in both her personal and professional life, staying true to her personal values, and speaking her truth. This is part of her North Node purpose. Up until now, she said, "It hasn't come easy for me as my biggest fear is what other people will think," which is her South Node tendency.

The realization that she was meant to resolve this within herself was acknowledged in her words during our first session together: "This has affirmed the difficult pieces of work that I need to do while feeling supported and confident that this is the time to do it, that the sun and the moon and the stars are aligned to help me." She was committed to doing the work, so we looked ahead at how the major cosmic energies in the upcoming astrological calendar would play out in her life. This helped her leverage opportunities toward her growth path.

Kim was a little hesitant at first. She didn't want to engage in anything that had a "fortune telling" vibe. She felt more comfortable when she understood how astrology can be used as a strategic tool for better planning and decision making in different areas of her life.

I describe the process as more a language of energy that, when effectively applied, an astrologer can read many possible effects some planetary influences can have on you in a holistic way. My approach is to read the energy within the context of my client's life so they can co-create the experience based on possible choices or opportunities presented to them. Astrology cannot predict exactly what will happen as free will always exists in our choices.

This approach allowed Kim to identify the potential highs and lows in different areas of her life that will come into her reality, and how she wants to co-create that experience. Through the next several sessions, she learned the best time to take action in her life and business (or when not to take action) to move her toward her North Node path and the overall desires and dreams for her life.

Over the course of the next several months, Kim made adjustments in her life and business. She had difficult conversations with people, realigned her business model with her personal brand values, declined work that was no longer in alignment, and readjusted travel plans, which allowed her to focus on family matters that may have otherwise caught her by surprise.

One of Kim's most recent professional accomplishments was the achievement of the Speaker of the Year award in a community she has served for the past several years. The announcement came when the North Node placement in her birth chart was "activated" by a planetary energy bringing about a time when others value and recognize you.

COME HOME TO THE POWER WITHIN YOU

When circumstances in our lives change or no longer work for us, we experience confusion, uncertainty, frustration, and an overall feeling of "stuck-ness." There's a natural tendency to seek answers outside of ourselves:

- We enroll in a program to learn something new.

- We hire a coach or mentor to help us figure it out.
- We look at others who are where we want to be.
- We ask a trusted friend for advice.

While all of the above play a role in helping us get to the next level of success, many of us rely too heavily on outside influences (or influencers). We spend a significant amount of time and money seeking answers outside of ourselves.

Why is that?

- We don't trust ourselves.
- We're running on the hamster wheel and can't be in stillness long enough to listen to our higher self.
- We think we are not good enough (or have a fear of failure).
- We don't go after what we truly want for fear of judgment of what others will think of us.

It took me 54 years to discover that the answers are within me. My birth chart, and working with the natural energies and cycles in the cosmos, are the most direct path to success, purpose and fulfillment. While I wish that I had learned all this when I was 30 years old, I believe this path was meant to lead me exactly where I am today.

The true power in reaching your next level of success lies in coming home to yourself. It's knowing who you are, the gifts you have been given to share, the purpose you are meant to live, and living in the fullest expression of your authentic self.

To express your authentic self, it may not always feel easy and clear to show up in your authenticity, but this work holds the key to your success, joy, meaningful relationships, passion, and purpose. You were born to be you—and no one else knows how to be you besides you. The power is within YOU.

When you're true to yourself, you build trust and credibility with your clients, your colleagues, your team, your family and friends. Being genuine and transparent allows people to see the real you and connect better with you.

Aligning with astrology is one of the most direct ways to express your authenticity and reach your highest potential with clarity, confidence, and courage. You will better understand who you are and your path to get there. You will be able to embody the fullest expression of yourself, live on-purpose with internal fulfillment, and reach success on your own terms.

Come home to the power within YOU!

To harness the power of your personal astrology and reach your next level of success, you can learn more on my website and schedule a complimentary call with me:

https://www.barbaracalexander.com

Robin Tasco

Robin, raised in Philadelphia, learned the value of hard work and determination at an early age. She is a Master electrician, certified electrical inspector and electrical plans examiner. She also teaches electrical DIY and electrical exam prep courses and is an Amazon best seller and a sought-after speaker on labor and women issues.

How to Stand Up to the Dark Side

Dealing with Misogyny, Racism and Envy in the Workplace

by Robin Tasco

I began my 30-year relationship with the Electrical Trades Union when it resided in the old Lits building in Philadelphia. Little did I know that this dank, dark place of old dreams and ghosts would eventually fill my heart, drain my soul, betray my love, and engage me in a push and pull of racism, sexism, and plain ol' stupidity.

Today I am a veteran member of the International Brotherhood of Electrical Workers (IBEW), but I will never forget my first steps into this complex union built on ideals of loyalty, skills, devotion, family, and fair pay... for white males. Since its inception in 1891, the latter has, unfortunately, become the other face of the IBEW which has since become a poster child picture of greed, intolerance, thuggery, racism, and corrupted power.

Philadelphia is a union town and what that actually means depends on who you're speaking to. If you are a politician, it can be a voting base that supports you no matter what as long as you help keep its members employed. If you are white, male (specifically Irish or Italian) it means your road to a steady job with good pay and benefits is a lot smoother than others who are not that— specifically black and brown people—but just as qualified. If you are a black, single, female with a young child looking for the key to financial stability and a better life, it is also a beacon of hope dimly shining behind a fog of challenges within and without.

My first day on the job at the Lit Brothers work site was as a seasonal helper for the Electrical Trades Union, a position one supervisor described as being "lower than whale shit." Still, it was with a mixture of awe, pride, and even a bit of intimidation that I stepped inside the historic structure to start a career that began with hope and enthusiasm for a future that looked, on that day, incredibly bright. I reverently handed over the slip of paper from the Union Hall to the man sitting at the desk inside.

"Good morning," he said. "My name is Joe."

"Hi Joe, my name is Robin," I replied and I shook his hand as firmly as he grasped mine. We left the trailer and I followed him to the job site.

There I found an army consisting mostly of Irish and Italians with a smattering of Poles and a few Blacks and even fewer Puerto Ricans. There was a small, barely noticeable sprinkling of women. I started work at 7 a.m. and by 9 a.m., the time set for coffee break, everyone at the site knew that a "girl by the name of Robin" was among them. By the end of the day, several had already asked questions like: "Are you related to someone? Do you know someone in this business? How did you find out about the electrical program?" These were not casual questions or small talk leading to a bigger conversation. What they really wanted to know was who sponsored me and how did I even get here. No one asked me if I had gotten a key to the women's porta-potty, or whether I remembered how to get to the material room, or whether they could help with a particularly heavy and/or awkward load of supplies.

Many—both black and white men—considered this type of work exclusively for men, and the very few times they encountered a woman who was not related or someone they didn't know who also happened to be black, it was a serious disturbance in the force. After only a couple of days, the inquiries elevated to accusations in the shape of questions, asking "Do you realize you're taking a job that a man should have?" or "Do you really think you'll? be able to last?" At the time, women on a job site was both a rarity and a threat to the male dominated union culture that guarded it like it was the door to nirvana.

I got hired as a seasonal helper recommended by the Urban Coalition, a nonprofit that acts as a pool for minority workers sought by the union. To be clear, there was no sense of fairness and/or benevolence from the unions that created this relationship with the Urban Coalition. Numerous lawsuits, political pressure, and most importantly, lucrative federal contracts that stated a certain number of minorities (depending on the size of the job) must be hired on 10 construction sites that took federal money, forced the unions to open their doors just a crack. Back then, I was one of the few people at the forefront of this losing battle for equality in the union workforce. As much as I was a welcome sight to those trying to breach the walls of racism and sexism, I was equally despised, minimized, and stereotyped by those working just as hard to keep it in place.

Before becoming a full member of the IBEW, I was out at this nightclub called, The Impulse, on a Friday night after a long, tiring week of lifting, bending, and fending off sexual advances and insults from co-workers. I love to dance and, like most women, love to dress well, socialize, and listen to music in a safe space that is about unwinding and simply having a good time more than anything else.

That was my frame of mind that night when I ran into one of the journeymen who worked on the site with me. Other than saying hi, I didn't pay him any mind at all and literally kept it moving. His name was "Bull" which was short for Bullock. I had seen him around and often overheard him complaining about his several children and how much he owed in child support and other negative drama in his life. He was a fairly attractive man and physically fit, but his personal life—by his own admission—always seemed to be in a state of disarray with many challenges.

Shortly after that night of "hi and bye", we went weeks with no real communication other than a nod or one word greeting, which was not unusual because there was never any real back-and-forth between us. Then one day, he asked me to get some material for him from the material shanny shop in a very nasty way. As a seasonal helper it was part of my job to fetch things for the journeyman without question. Though I sometimes found it annoying, never, until that moment, had anyone—white or black—spoken to me in such a disrespectful way.

Before I could catch myself, I responded just as nasty and loud that he had no right to speak to me in such a condescending and gruff manner and he and I began to loudly go back-and-forth as others looked on. Eventually common sense got the best of me and I walked away in the midst of the exchange. He called after me saying, "Don't nobody ignore the Bull!!!"

Perplexed by the comment, I responded a bit calmer that he had no right to treat me with disrespect even if I basically just ran errands. To my surprise, my status had nothing to do with his bad behavior. He said that the night he saw me at the club I had ignored him because I didn't stop to chat. I asked him if he was serious because I couldn't believe he had been holding onto a slight I had no idea I had committed. Literally puffing out his chest, he explained that he was indeed serious and again that, "Don't nobody ignore The Bull."

I found the whole thing so absurd that I began to laugh. "When I'm out," I explained as if I were talking to a pouting child, "I am out on my own time as an adult, and you need to get over yourself." I then walked away to get the materials he needed. It never got any deeper than that, and in fact, when I ran into him years later, we both joked about the incident. Honestly, it was mild compared to other encounters that would follow.

A few months into the job, John, the general foreman, wanted my help with payroll time sheets for a few hours a day. It was unusual to take a person in my humble position and put them in such a responsible place, but contractors work with any tool that fits the job and tend to look at people the same way. I had put on my application that I had some minimal experience in accounting at a previous job and I guess after reading that, they saw me as the hammer for that particular nail. I later learned the person who normally did this was fired because he was messing up paychecks by recording the incorrect number of hours a person worked. It was supposed to be for just a few hours a day but turned into all day every day.

Though I had nowhere near the knowledge of a full-fledged accountant, I only needed to get the numbers right at this level which earned me some respect and lifted me a few inches above the shit at the bottom of the sea. Again, this move off the site and into the office was unexpected, not only because of my lowly status, but also because I was only one of three black women working there. The other two were Cheryl, a second-year apprentice who wasn't very friendly, and Linda, with whom I eventually formed a lukewarm relationship.

Instead of offering advice on helping to get me through this first mile of the way, I wasn't offered so much as a glimpse of the compass and was pretty much left on my own. I just accepted it for what it was and kept moving. I had other pressing responsibilities that included a child to feed and clothe and bills that didn't care whether Cheryl or Linda believed in sisterhood. I was also still dealing with the everyday nonsense of aggressive flirts, nasty whispers, while filtering conversations with men who were genuinely nice and trying to help, as opposed to those wanting to get into my pants with the deliberate speed of someone wagering a bet.

In fact, one of the first things mentioned to me at the Lit Brothers site by several men I had just met was to stay away from Cheryl and Linda because they were "trouble." Trouble. The same word I heard throughout my life when a woman went somewhere or did something that was supposed to be reserved for males. Trouble was the last thing on my mind. Survival was the first.

EDUCATION IS KEY

However, the unofficial job of keeping track of time cards did put me in a position to find out what it would take to get into the apprenticeship program. When I finished the five-year, college accredited, apprenticeship course in 1992 and officially became a journeyman/certified electrician, I felt proud of myself for reaching such a milestone. Finishing such a rigorous program lifted my spirits and pride, and though it didn't take away all the baggage, it helped me unload enough to move forward with more confidence than ever. The frustration, loneliness, disappointment, depression, and emotional scars that accumulated along the journey to achieving full union status would take years to heal and will never be forgotten. Neither will the pride, and hard-earned knowledge of myself and my determination to succeed.

Though the sexism came from both black and white men, it was the latter that held a distinct type of toxic beliefs so deeply embedded in their cultural DNA that even they didn't understand where it came from and why it seemed impossible to escape. I began to mentally catalog each challenge and experience and used it to catapult me to the next opportunity. I also learned to read through the simple-mindedness of racism by understanding the fear at its base which became only as great as I allowed it to be.

For example, there were times when white men at a work site would show compassion, treat me as an equal or even muster the courage to compliment me on the quality of my work. Though such actions may have elevated their status as humans, it lowered their position as a white male in the eyes of their peers because they dared to express a simple courtesy to a female whose skin just happened to be a different color. They even invented a phrase for it a hundred years ago that exists to this day: "Ni…r lover."

On a different scale but no less harmful, a few black union men I've met over the years had their own club based on the same set of baseless notions. They shared the same beliefs as their white male counterparts when it came to black women standing on equal union ground with equal/greater skills who were striving for the coveted union card. This family dysfunction is systemic in many unions when it comes to sexism and race. Those shortchanged because of the color of their skin sometimes inflict that pain on someone else they MUST consider lower than they are, in order to have any status at all.

When I came through my apprenticeship, there were no other black women going through at the same time. I had one white woman in my class and she and I were pretty cool. She worked for the union before formally getting in as a union member. She received the kind of help, support, and encouragement throughout her apprenticeship that I rarely experienced.

When I started in the electrical apprenticeship program, the instructors were exactly that, instructors, not teachers. The apprenticeship program was as rigorous as any college course and, in fact, was generally viewed as a college-level program by academicians. There was plenty of classroom work as well as complex homework assignments you had a week to figure out before the next weekly class. Homework was more than enough to carry you to the next class. Most in the program had family members who had already gone through. This nepotism continues to be a major reason large local unions like the IBEW remain predominantly white.

Still, the first year I, along with several others, flunked the class. For me, it wasn't the academics so much as how the class was taught versus how I was taught to learn. The way it was served made it hard to understand each problem, not the actual problem itself. During these strenuous classes I was still being exposed to the uglier side of union culture. It was not unusual for me to be called the "N" word from across the room. It was always said loud enough for me to hear but at a distance too far to identify the culprit, but all the men in that area were white.

One day, I got on a freight elevator crowded with white tradesmen at Lit Brothers and as I looked around, I noticed one of the men wearing a keychain hanging from his belt hoop with the letters KKK on it. I later found out that his name was Ray and he was an electrician. This was in 1987 not 1957. I really couldn't believe what I was seeing. I didn't see the keychain until after I was already on the crowded elevator of about 12 people; and everywhere I looked someone was staring at me, like they were trying to read my thoughts. I had already experienced and seen plenty of ignorance and stupidity, but I was still shocked to see such a blatant display of it. I grew up in a diverse neighborhood. I had white kids as classmates and I interacted with white people regularly. However, working on that job with mostly white men, it was my first up close experience with racism presented as if it were as normal as breathing. Fortunately, Ray proved to be the exception and not the rule.

I used to struggle with the why and how that motivates someone to do something so blatantly wrong and disrespectful and do it so casually. Where were the moral checks and balances? Why didn't one of his friends say something like: "Bruh! You know that ain't right." At some point I realized no such checks and balances exist because there is no pressure or light shone on a culture that keeps such despicable behavior invisible from the public and sometimes uses it to keep power in place and the money flowing.

I first met John Dougherty on the Lit Brothers job site in 1987. He was a young journeyman at the time with a passion for politics and an ideology that was reflected in his work dress of American-made construction boots, jeans, and chambray shirt. He came off as an "every man." He was someone with an aura of commonality that got your attention because it seemed authentic. He also didn't show any overt signs of sexism or racism in his demeanor. He always had a smile and was congenial but didn't linger for much chit chat beyond the basics of, "Hi, how you doing," or "Good to see you again. Hope all is well."

By the time Johnny became Business Manager, he was recognized as an up-and coming union leader with plenty of passion and a talent for maneuvering through the massive amounts of bullshit from politicians, contractors, and even union members seeking a seat at the table he now owned. It was a heady position that demanded the kind of respect and fealty that usually comes with absolute power. I saw him go from wearing white socks with nothing but American-made shoes, to dressing like a Wall Street player as he began to favor Armani over Sears. He began wearing shirts and ties from Boyd's (one of the most exclusive and expensive men's clothing shops in Philadelphia) and those didn't come in plastic wrapping.

Of course, like most in powerful positions, he had an entourage that floated around him like butterflies. They consisted mostly of handpicked, all white, male business agents whose positions came with cars, money, and power—all made possible by 5,000 dues-paying workers. That money was also used to make sure union contractors got jobs they wouldn't have been able to afford to bid for if they were under bid by a non-union contractor. The difference in whatever money the union contractor would've lost by putting in an equally low bid was given to the union contractor by IBEW and was never paid back. The amount could range from a few thousand to hundreds of thousands of dollars that was simply funneled somewhere else... and disappeared.

CLIMBING THE LADDER

In 1992, I graduated from the apprentice program (or "topped out" as we called it) while working onsite at the Pennsylvania Convention Center in Philadelphia. I was now an official journeyman in the IBEW after five long years of college-level academics, hard labor, ceaseless crude, sexist comments and encountering racism at even the most benign levels of engagement. I was very proud of what I had accomplished (I even got the "most improved" student award), and, in some corner of my own reasoning, I assumed that gaining full membership would lift me to a level above the ignorance and place me on equal ground with my union brothers and sisters.

While at the Convention Center I was partnered with a former business agent who had been returned to the field once Johnny won the coveted Business Manager spot. This was neither unusual nor punitive. It wasn't much different than the shift in power that occurs when any elected official takes office and moves her own people in as an incumbent moves out. My partner's brother was also a longtime financial secretary for the local and word was out that he was looking to retire. I remember telling my partner that the financial secretary position was something I'd be interested in doing. His reply, which caught me off guard, was straightforward and plain: "That's a man's job. You can't do that." He said it without even thinking about it. Like it was some well-known fact and was OK to say because just as we know water is wet and birds fly, a position of financial secretary in a union is a "man's job."

Here was a guy I had been working with for about six months, and who treated me decently and with respect. Now, suddenly, I heard a voice speaking from a different dimension of "normal" that was apparently accepted in this other space as gospel. This sub-culture of power had its own rules and reality that only revealed itself once you crossed one of those invisible lines and/or you made yourself visible by speaking out for or against something that could disturb this sacred space.

On the surface, it was mostly smiles, congeniality, and compassion... as long as your issues remained unseen, and their white fragility was never disturbed. Returning from the shanty with the material that had been requested by two men, I delivered it to the first journeyman simply because I had to go past him to get to George, who saw me dropping off the material. He started to scream at me about the amount of time I took to get back to him.

Before I could explain to him what I was doing, he walked away still fussing and called me a "bitch." I couldn't believe what I was hearing. I looked at the other journeyman who was standing nearby and heard the comment. He also seemed to be in disbelief as he tried to calm me down because I was visibly upset. There is a trigger, I think, in most people that clicks when something egregious is done to them or someone crosses a line that is cast in cement and immovable. For me, the line was crossed when I was called a "bitch."

I went to the dumpster and found a 2x4 wooden stick and went looking for George. When I found him I told him that if he ever spoke to me like that again I was gonna take this stick and shove it up his ass. All of this back-and-forth spirited language got the attention of the shop steward. He and I then told the general foreman for the site about what happened and why. The foreman was also George's buddy. After explaining what happened and the steward telling George he could not talk to me that way, the resolution was to simply remove me and put me in another gang. No reprimand for George. No warning. No nothing. The solution to the problem was apparently to place the cloak of invisibility once again on the victim by removing her presence from the union's line of sight.

In the new gang, I was put on a chopping concrete detail. Yes. I didn't stutter... a chopping concrete detail!! I was given a TE 72 hammer gun with a chopping bit that came up to my hip. I'm only 5'2" tall, and had never worked with any power tool that was half the length of my body. It was also very heavy and unwieldy and could cause serious bodily harm if used improperly. Ironically, it was exactly the kind of tool one would think, "only a man could use," and yet here I was taking on this challenge as if I was built like "the Bull."

No matter where I was put during my time at IBEW, I managed to make the best of any bad situation and learn something from it. As for the "stick in the ass" event, George also learned something that day about lines and a black woman on a mission. The comment cost me in physical work, but it was an invoice I paid willingly.

One day, I was doing my paperwork in our lunch trailer when I overheard some of the guys in the back of the trailer talking about a woman being on all fours and what they wanted to do to her in that position. I couldn't believe what I was hearing. I pulled my stuff together and left the trailer in disgust. The next day, I went back to the trailer to have my lunch, and just as I took out my food they started with the same conversation and now I knew it was being done on purpose and meant to be loud enough for me to hear. I decided to walk back there to confront them about their offensive comments. I said to Gene, the shop steward who was sitting with the group making the comment, that I needed to speak to him. He knew what I wanted so he took his sweet time getting to me. I asked him if he thought it was appropriate for these guys to have this conversation while I am having my lunch in the same trailer? His reply was I can't tell these guys how to talk when they are having lunch.

The drug of empowerment also shaped their minds to believe that electrician jobs should be the exclusive domain of white men. So, I made a phone call to the business office and left a message with the business agent telling him that I was having a problem down at the job site at 36th and Chestnut Streets. I needed him to come out and deal with it or there was going to be a serious problem. The steward, as in all unions, is supposed to be the person who represents you and your concerns with any union entity in a workspace that is treating you unfairly. He or she is also to act as a mediator in that same space. This also applies to fellow union members.

The steward and I were friendly, and we also kidded with each other with no issues. I mention it because my feelings at the time of this incident were a swirling mix of betrayal, disappointment, and a creeping recognition that no matter what I did nor how hard I worked I wondered if I would ever be treated with the respect I deserved. I was a full journeyman at this time and that special place in my heart was formed from their school of hard knocks where I paid my academic, physical, and psychological dues two times over, showed up faithfully, and did the work required of me.

Yet, none of that seemed to matter in this moment because the complaint was immediately perceived as a threat to this ignorant good ol' boy network of white men feeling privileged enough to dismiss your humanity because you are a black woman with no status they felt obligated to recognize. Again, the steward's job is to remain neutral in any dispute until a fact-gathering investigation is done and based on their decisions/recommendations alone. In this case, those I complained against were all his buddies and charter members of "the club " The business agent came down that day and spoke to the steward before talking to us together. I explained what I heard during my lunch in the trailer the first day and how I simply left to get away from it. When it happened again the next day, I knew it was intentional, so I followed protocol and complained to the steward who was sitting with the group that made the offensive comments.

At the end of the discussion between the business agent, myself, and the steward, the steward was told that no profanity or explicit language could be spoken in front of me, or any woman on any job site. The business agent also ordered all of their pin up go-go girls with their breasts hanging out and legs wide open to be taken out of all the gang box(es) or changing areas. The decision proved to be a two-edged sword because even though the offensive pictures were taken down, it was interpreted by the men as being unfair. They felt that if Robin couldn't handle the language, profanity and tastes in pictures then she shouldn't be on a job site.

TRYING TO MOVE UP

When I began working on staff in 2001 for Local 98 as a Black Union Representative, I not only made history for the electricians' union but for the entire Philadelphia building trades. I was the first black woman to represent the Philadelphia Building Trades and the first Black Union Representative of a mechanical trade. I was also doing the same type of work for (and even more) than any of the other union representatives on this administrative team. However, I was still getting paid less than my white colleagues. However, I was making journeyman's wages but working like I was part of management on a salary and was only getting 40 hours of wages.

To be clear, I had been asking Johnny for quite some time about getting equal pay for the position and he pretty much just blew me off. After close to five years of being paid less than the position called for, Johnny agreed to pay me at the Business Representative rate, and all it took was a phone call. Meanwhile, some of the Black Union members thought that my position was a joke despite all the hard work I put in and the fact I had earned a reputation for deflating potentially volatile situations and ensuring that work went to our guys on a regular basis. Also, some in the black community considered Johnny a racist and was just using me as his token black. Of course, I didn't like these perceptions but I also understood some of it was because they couldn't get to Johnny so they took out their frustrations and bitter feelings on me simply because I was both approachable and the only face of IBEW they could recognize besides Johnny's.

This all came to a head in a meeting filled with white men that Johnny was trying to impress. Hearing his conversation, I just wanted to leave the room, but apparently he saw the anguish on my face because he later asked me what was wrong. I told him I didn't want to talk about it, but he insisted and said he didn't have time for me to pout. My mind was so full of both penetrating and conflicting thoughts, that I blurted out: "I am not your token!" Johnny turned beet red and started going back-and-forth about what he had done for me, and I in turn told him how hard I'd worked for the team and how little respect and acknowledgement I received for my efforts. The next day, I was called into his office for a meeting with him and the assistant business manager. He was obviously still very upset as he told me that he was "done with me."

The Robin Tasco of today can still kick it with the best of the electricians and I continue to teach at every opportunity. My journey of 30 years of being associated with the IBEW as both management and laborer has been as exciting as it has been disappointing and as enlightening as it has, at times, been discouraging. Still, I wouldn't take anything for the journey thus far. I continue to feel blessed to have overcome the challenges with the same energy I battled the ignorance and intolerance of the people still clinging to a belief that white is superior to black and male is superior to female. While the changes I was able to bring about were often small and incremental, they were still positive changes, and I will continue to lift my feet and walk in that direction.

ABOUT THE AUTHOR

Robin Tasco is an Electrician with over 30 years of experience in the construction industry. She was the first women Union Business Agent of the IBEW Local Union 98 and Union Representative of the Philadelphia Building Trade, a Master Electrician and a Licensed Electrical Inspector. She is also an Owner and CEO of Tasco's Contractors Inc. She is married to Will Tasco, Jr and they have four sons Frank, Triaz, Moses, and Lucky and one daughter, Lauren.

Robin is currently creating courses, looking for speaking opportunities, and will soon be launching a podcast on how women can effectively, efficiently, and positively continue the fight against misogyny, racism, and envy in the workplace.

A sense of belonging is something so personal and sensitive that it is very hard to get meaningful feedback, but together we can create a world where barriers are the things of the past. For speaking and or talks visit my linktr.ee to schedule a time.

https://calendly.com/robtasco

Mindy Scarlett

SCARLETT CREATIVE GROUP / PARTNER IN THE CENTER OF INFLUENCE COMMUNITY

Mindy brings her 30 years of experience in branding, marketing, and ghostwriting to help coaches, consultants, and thought leaders write bestselling books that shine a light on their brand, gain visibility, and increase revenue.

Know When to Pull the Ripcord

by Mindy Scarlett

When I started writing a paper on the advertising methods of The Coca-Cola Company in my sophomore year in college, I had no idea I was laying the groundwork for a major change that would divert the entire trajectory of the rest of my life, both personally and professionally. I was enjoying my second year at a small private university in southern Michigan, I had a wide circle of friends, and I went home most weekends to do my laundry at mom's house. I was living the life of a carefree college student who knew where she was going (or I sure thought I did!)

I was majoring in marketing and public relations, had to do a term paper. I decided to focus on analyzing whether the advertising of The Coca-Cola Company followed changes in society or did they cause them? I had done all the research and had written out my paper longhand, but my professors had begun making it mandatory that all term papers needed to be typed. I had used an electric typewriter all through high school and was tired of having to fiddle with whiteout to make corrections.

At this point in history, the concept of personal computers and word processors was just beginning to emerge, and I found it necessary to go to the Writing Center on campus to get help with using the Commodore 64-word processors that used floppy disks. The manager of the Writing Center was an Australian master's-level student who took a shine to me, helping me with the computer issues and advising me on my term paper. He kept asking me out, and I kept insisting that I was only interested in friendship. Over the remainder of the year, he finally convinced me that we should be more than friends and after we started going out, the mantra changed to the tune of we should get married and I should immigrate to Melbourne with him, sight unseen.

I finally capitulated, and I saw this as an adventure, packed up three suitcases and a steamer trunk and proceeded to drive across the U.S. before catching a Qantas flight to Melbourne. This was my first time out of the continental U.S., and my inexperience at traveling showed up in a very inconvenient way when I misread the tickets by not factoring in the international date line. This meant that my introduction to my in-laws was them standing at the airport waiting for us, and we did not arrive until 24 hours later! (This was the days before cell phones, so it took quite some time to get it sorted out.)

So, I was beginning marriage in a foreign country where my spouse was the only person that I knew, I had not completed my college degree, I was on the hunt for a job, and we were living in a camper van in my in-laws' front garden! I was determined to "make a go" of both my marriage and living in Australia and threw myself into creating a home and a life for both of us. I soon found a job (and so did he), and we were able to move into our own apartment and buy a 1969 white VW beetle as a form of transportation. Luckily, this was only needed for weekend trips, as I could get to work on the extensive tramway system in Melbourne.

Working conditions in Australia are second to none. The first year I was there, I took a four-week holiday to go back and see my family, and everyone thought I had quit my job! I had to assure them that in the land down under, everyone got four weeks' annual leave from year one no matter what industry they worked in. We also got over two and half weeks of public holidays, very generous sick leave and the amazing concept of a nine-day fortnight! (Simply put, that means if you only take a 30-minute lunch break every day, you can collect the additional time and have every other Friday off from work!)

So, it was at the grand old age of 20 that I began my initial dive into the Australian corporate world, starting with a short-lived job with the ad agency J. Walter Thompson where I lasted all of three months. I had taken on the position of secretary to an account management group, thinking I could work my way into a creative position. It soon became apparent that I was NOT cut out to be a secretary, and there was NOT a trail to be blazed into the creative department as secretaries were expected to stay secretaries!

Being an American in Melbourne actually turned out to be a good thing. My accent made me stand out, and I was able to get good jobs even though I had not finished my degree. Three years after arriving in Australia, I landed a job at the Peter MacCallum Cancer Institute. They were happy to send me back to school, and after moving on to a job at National Mutual as manager of the newly created Desktop Publishing Department, I finally graduated with my BA in public relations with a minor in business.

Working for National Mutual was an amazing experience. I was delighted to be working for a corporation that truly appreciated my talents and experience, and who basically gave me a blank check to buy the technology necessary to set up a state-of-the-art department. I happily began buying the best tech and hiring support staff to create what was essentially an in-house advertising agency. We were responsible for creating the artwork for flyers, booklets and brochures for the various departments within the superannuation and pension division of the company.

As desktop publishing was a new thing, the company was not sure where to put it and initially placed my department in the corporate structure under the Computer Systems Group. My manager, Kevin Campbell, was a great mentor to me as I learned how to be a manager and how to play the corporate game of politics. He had plenty of "sage" advice and was very even handed in how he dealt with people.

After a year of building the department and establishing a reputation for creating great work in a more than timely manner, management began to notice. There was a Corporate Communications Department that often used our services, and management thought it would be a good idea to merge the two departments, as I was providing graphics and writing services, not computer services, which made it more than a little awkward being part of the Computer Systems area. I had become friendly with one of the senior staff members in the Communications area, and she was delighted with the concept of the two departments merging.

At this time I was still in my twenties, and I still had a lot to learn about human nature. Let me put it this way—there is a reason why I don't play poker, and it's because you can tell what I'm thinking just by looking at me! I thought I had formed a friendship with the senior consultant from the Corporate Communications Department and that she was looking forward to working with me in the newly merged department.

On one hand, it looked like a dream come true to be invited to be the manager of a newly created department. The new position came with an office with a view, a slightly higher paycheck and a company car. I felt I was truly on my way to climbing the corporate ladder, and eventually, I would have the opportunity to break the glass ceiling.

However, when I was put in place as the manager of the merged departments, I soon found out that I did NOT have a friendship with the senior communications consultant—I now had an enemy who felt I had stolen her promotion! I was blindsided and totally unsure how to deal with the situation. This consultant had a close relationship with one of our major clients, and she began to vent to them about how unfair it was that I had been given the management position over her, and this caused the higher ups to be concerned about the tempest in a teapot that was brewing with one of their major clients.

I was called in by the head of our division to see how I was going to handle the situation. I assured him that I was dealing with it and moved the client in question to another consultant. I, however, still had to deal with an openly hostile staff member. Upper management's reaction to this was to instruct me to fire her.

While to Americans that seems like a short and sweet way to deal with a difficult situation, in Australia it is an entirely different thing! The only way you can fire someone on the spot is if they are caught doing something criminal. Otherwise, there is a long and tedious process for firing anyone. You must send them a letter stating what activities they need to "cease and desist" with a timeframe for compliance. Then, the manager must track activity every day and keep a log of any activities that do not comply. Next, another letter must be issued, stating all the incidences of noncompliance, and giving yet another warning followed by a compliance timeline. Then, and only then, after many months of negative "back and forth," can you actually fire the person in question.

I had neither the heart nor the temperament to go through this tedious and negative process, that would have created a hostile environment for everyone in the department. While I did not appreciate how she was dealing with the situation, I could understand how she felt. The whole situation surrounding the merging of the two departments had not been handled properly from the top down, and I was now dealing with the fallout. However, by this time, my relationship with her was so tattered that I truly felt that I could not repair it enough to continue as her manager, but at the same time I was not prepared to get rid of her the "hard way."

This left me in the ultimate Catch 22 situation, and it felt like I had nowhere to go. By this time, my mentor/manager had succumbed to corporate intrigue and had been unseated in a coup that left him without a seat. The head of the division was a big, burly man who did not want any warm and fuzzy meetings; he just wanted results. As the situation continued, the stress it created had begun to take its toll on every aspect of my life. I started getting sick, I was always tired, and it seemed that no matter how hard I tried, I could never get to the end of my to-do list as I had a senior staff member I could no longer depend on.

After months of high stress levels and with repeated pressure from management to "get rid of" my difficult staff member, I finally came up with an idea. While the path to firing someone for cause was long and difficult, there was another way; they could be made redundant. Simply put, a company can say they have too many of a certain type of staff member and then let them go. However, there are very strict rules surrounding this, and the staff member must be given a "golden handshake" that coincides with the number of years that they had worked for the company.

So, I walked into the division manager's office and announced that I was stepping down as manager to become a Senior Communication Consultant and that management could use this fact as a way to make the troublesome staff member redundant, rather than trying to fire her for cause and getting into a major legal wrangle, which could have ended up in a wrongful dismissal lawsuit.

Management took me up on the idea, and I cooperated in every way possible, from helping to draft the ad to look for a new manager to sitting in on the interviews. Their final choice was an older woman named Patty, who was an absolute dream to work with and was very supportive of my decision to stay on in the department. I helped her in every way that I could to come aboard, get acquainted with the entire department and keep things on an even keel.

However, the months of high stress had taken their toll, and even though Patty and I had a great working relationship, I began to really question my decision to stay. I began to network and acquire some freelance clients on the side and after six months, I handed in my resignation to step out and begin my own public relations company.

Patty was amazing. She supported my decision, was fine with me giving one month's notice and even began using me as a freelancer for overspill work after I left. I quickly gathered several more clients and then went on to acquire my first ghostwriting contract. I had established an amazing home office in the country about an hour north of Melbourne, I was making good money and everything was starting to look great—everything, that is, except my marriage.

While I was climbing the corporate ladder and beginning to earn some serious money, my husband was still stuck in contract teacher mode. What this meant was he only got paid for nine months of the year. So, I had to earmark any extra money I earned and put it to one side to ensure we could pay bills for the three months every year when he did not bring home a paycheck. It was also up to me to put money aside for major projects like updates to our home.

Being the absent professor type, my husband would spend these three months reading, studying and eventually writing, both articles and books. Unfortunately, none of these pursuits actually produced any income. By being very careful with money, I was able to bridge the gap, but it also meant that we were not able to save much. And the agreement had been that if I immigrated, that I would get to come home every year to see my family. While that is a wonderful sentiment (and I enjoyed the three weeks at home each year), it also was a hefty investment in plane tickets and holiday money.

Even with all these financial challenges, we finally managed to buy a house in the small town of Woodend, about an hour north of Melbourne. There was an amazing rail system, and I was able to commute back and forth on the train most days. There was a whole group of people who lived in the small towns around Woodend, and we soon formed a social club of sorts!

By the time we hit our 10-year anniversary, my husband was still a contract teacher. I began to be a bit concerned and decided it was time to start planning for retirement. I began a 401K at work and began to make plans for other investments.

In the meantime, my husband was working on a book on the history of the Windsor Hotel, a grand European-style hotel in downtown Melbourne. I very much wanted to help him with it, but he was too egotistical to even listen to any of my suggestions, so in the interest of peace, I left him to his long stints of research, either at the library or in his study at home.

After the bout of corporate burnout, I was quite proud of the fact that I kept the company I had just resigned from as a client and began adding others. One of my clients was a friend who owned a local winery who was also interested in alternative medicine, and I got my first experience as a book ghostwriter. (Contrary to my husband's opinion of my writing skills, other people were willing to pay for them!)

My husband, however, seemed to be going deeper and deeper into absent-minded professor mode. I was the one going out on weekends, while he stayed behind on his newly acquired computer, researching and writing. His book on the Windsor Hotel was finally published. It was a lovely hardcover book and when I turned the pages and read the three pages of acknowledgments, my heart stopped. He had thanked everyone in his life – except me! Nowhere was there even a mention that he was married! I was hurt, I was appalled, and it was a wake-up call.

Shortly after that I found a cartoon that showed a woman carrying an anniversary cake that had three layers. The bottom layer said, "First five years of marriage great," the second tier said, "The next five years so-so" and the final tier said, "Last few months: really bad." I showed my husband this cartoon and said that this was how I was feeling, and I thought that we should see a professional to help get our relationship back on track.

His response to this was to say he felt it was already too late to do anything about our relationship, and he had already made plans to return to the U.S. to begin work on his next book. He then went onto say he thought that I should continue to live at the house (of course this meant that I would be paying the mortgage) while he was dashing around writing books and looking for another place to live.

I was leaving the next day on a business trip to Sydney as I had a client who was launching a book, and I had an entire weekend of media coverage to handle and a book launch to execute. Thankfully, I was able to keep my composure together, and the press loved the new book. Like a robot, I kept putting one foot in front of the other, with a fixed smile plastered on my face, not at all sure of what I was going to do when I got back home.

I arrived back at the house in Woodend, and after a few nights of sleeping on the sofa, I rented an apartment and moved out of the house. I kept my head down and worked night and day for the Work and Family Life agency that was my main client. When they decided to make the position I was covering permanent, I applied. However, someone with more experience in book sales "scooped the pool," and I was passed over. This was the last straw, and I decided that it was time to return to the U.S. where my family would be ready, willing and able to support me, both financially and emotionally. So, I packed up my original three suitcases, liquidated my 401K to buy a plane ticket, and headed back to the good 'ole USA.

In my mind, I was returning home to the country that I had grown up in. Reality, however, was much different! Everyone had an accent, I was handling green money again (Australian money is very colorful, almost as if it comes from a Monopoly game), and I found that I was at an extreme disadvantage as I had no work history in the U.S. to speak of as well as no credit rating. The bottom line was that I did not exist as an adult in the U.S. I had never applied for a credit card, owned a car, or done any of the other things that people do to create a credit profile. I was lucky that I had a supportive family. My brother was a car dealer, and he handed me the keys to a loaner car and told me to keep it as long as I needed to. I couched-surfed between my parent's house and my brother's house while I looked for work.

I could not believe that I was 30 years old and starting over in every sense of the word. I had lost everything, my marriage, my business, my circle of friends – and I was in what initially felt like a foreign country, trying to figure out how to survive. The first work I found was as a freelance writer for the South Bend Tribune and the South Bend Executive Journal. The only problem was, I did not own a computer. Luckily, I had a friend from college who still lived nearby, and she was gracious enough to offer the use of her computer so that I could earn some money. I will be forever grateful to the female bank manager who finally took pity on me and gave me a loan for $500 to buy a computer to start my credit rating. Soon after that, I was able to get a car loan and move to Chicago where I rented my own apartment. This accomplishment took me two years to achieve, and because I was still working freelance, my income was still not stable.

However, living in Chicago gave me access to a wider network, and I soon landed a job as the PR manager for a non-profit organization. I began to relax and enjoy the new job, but soon learned that the manager who had hired me (and who was very supportive) had decided to take a new position at another company. This left me to deal with the egotistical male CEO who had very little time for women.

I soon found myself back on track for corporate burnout yet again! This CEO also put me in the position of having to fire someone, and he was unhappy when I did it, as I gave the poor person six weeks in which to find a new position. The CEO began nitpicking at everything I wrote and criticizing my every move. He then decided to replace the manager who had originally hired me, bringing in a woman who seemed to be more on an even keel.

However, I still had not learned my lesson about playing poker. I thought that being a woman that she would understand my struggles with the CEO, when in fact she used the things I had shared in confidence as a reason to justify firing me after I had only been on the job four months. I finally took this as a sign from the universe that I was NOT supposed to work for a corporation (or for anyone else) and I went back to being a freelancer. This put me on a path to learning the difference between being self-employed and actually owning a business.

Being self-employed means you work for yourself, like a one-person show. You call the shots, find your own clients, and handle all the work. When you're self-employed, you're on the hook for everything. If anything goes wrong, it's all on you. As a self-employed person, you earn money directly from your clients or customers—the only issue is that when you stop working, the income stops!

After meeting my current husband and moving to New Jersey, I was able to establish a small marketing agency that was quite successful. I learned the power of working with other people, instead of being a self-employed individual. I learned the power of going beyond just trading time for money and establishing a solid business by working with a great team.

The bottom line is this—there is no job on earth that is worth losing your health, peace of mind or personal relationships for, and it is imperative to know when to pull the ripcord. For the sake of perceived security, I went back to a J.O.B. when I came back to the U.S, even though I had taken the plunge of diving into self-employment while in Australia.

We have all been brainwashed at some point to accept that the safe route is to have a job with medical benefits, corner offices and company cars. However, all these items can become golden handcuffs, keeping us at the grind for longer than is necessary at a detriment to every aspect of our lives because we all like to have security even if it is only a "perceived" benefit.

Yes, in a perfect world, you do need to make plans and have a financial security blanket before pulling the ripcord and jumping from a steady job. However, we cannot always pick and choose what happens to us—sometimes life just takes over. So, whether you jump or are pushed, it is possible to create the financial security you crave by establishing a business in an area that you are passionate about. While it is an old saying, it is still true—do what you love, and the money will follow!

POINTS TO PONDER

Climbing the corporate ladder and breaking the glass ceiling is not for everyone. Some people thrive on it and find a way to go from rung to rung in a positive manner. However, if you are in an environment where positive change is impossible, then it might be time to explore what options exist beyond the corporate ladder.

Working for a small business or a nonprofit can provide a different environment and still provide the perceived security of a steady job. Changing from a hostile corporate environment does not need to mean you have to "start your own thing." It just means you need a change, if your environment is affecting all the other aspects of your life.

However, if you feel that you have the experience, the fortitude, and the resilience to "pull the ripcord" and step out on your own, then make a careful plan. This plan should include you creating your own brand, deciding on what your "super" power is, and putting together a business plan that clearly outlines how your business will be structured, who are your potential clients and exactly how you are going to make money.

If you are contemplating creating your own business, or if you have already launched and you want to write a best-selling book (or be in an Anthology!) to shine a light on your brand, then let's have that conversation! Text me at 908-499-9298 or book a call at:

https://tinyurl.com/mindyscarlett

www.ingramcontent.com/pod-product-compliance
Lightning Source LLC
Chambersburg PA
CBHW071357120626
46546CB00002B/728